WILLIAM C. RICE is head of the department of music at Baker University in Baldwin, Kansas. He also serves as minister of music at the First Methodist Church in Baldwin.

He received his education at the Conservatory of Music in Warrensburg, Missouri; State Teachers' College (B.S.) in Warrensburg; Northwestern University (M.Mus.) in Evanston, Illinois; and State University of Iowa (Ph.D.) in Iowa City.

In addition to having written numerous magazine articles, Dr. Rice is co-author of *Music and Worship in the Church* and *Vocal Technique for Children and Youth* and author of *Basic Principles of Singing*.

A CONCISE
HISTORY
OF
CHURCH
MUSIC

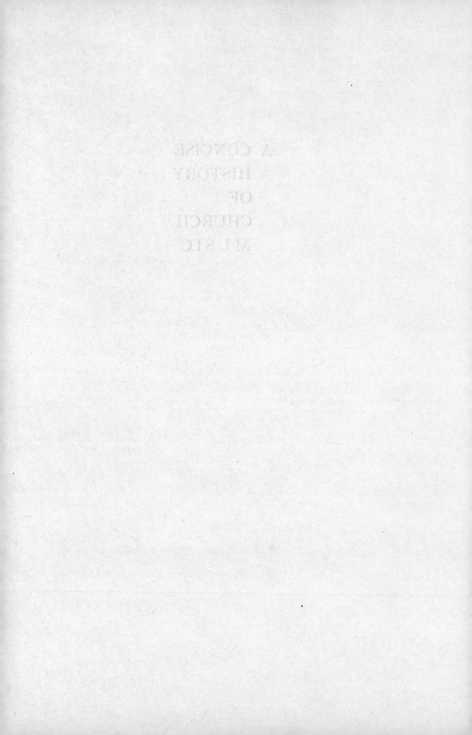

# A CONCISE HISTORY OF CHURCH MUSIC

William C. Rice

Abingdon Press    NEW YORK    NASHVILLE

A CONCISE HISTORY OF CHURCH MUSIC

Copyright © 1964 by Abingdon Press

Library of Congress Catalog Card Number: 64-10680

SET UP, PRINTED, AND BOUND BY THE
PARTHENON PRESS, AT NASHVILLE,
TENNESSEE, UNITED STATES OF AMERICA

# Preface

Church music is suffering from severe growing pains. Interest in the development of an effective program of church and church-school music was, until recently, limited to a few more or less well-trained musicians, fewer ministers, and even fewer educators. The present trend is toward involving all who are directly or indirectly affected by church music in the exciting and disturbing exploration of the contributions music can make to the total life of the church. One result of this broadening area of influence has been the discovery by many good churchmen that their knowledge about church music, and especially about church-music history, is embarrassingly deficient. Many who possess adequate technical skills in such areas as conducting, vocal and keyboard techniques, and organizational procedures are often lacking in their understanding of music history.

A Concise History of Church Music grew out of the pressing need for a brief, nontechnical, reliable discussion of the most important persons and the significant events that have brought church music to its present state of enthusiastic experimentation. Because so very much information had to be left out, more time and energy were spent in careful evaluation and re-evaluation of materials than in the actual writing of the book. My intention has been to trace the main stream of church music from its earliest beginnings and to bring in only those secondary streams that made significant contributions to its growth. Time will tell whether or not this intention has been realized partially, entirely, or not at all.

—WILLIAM C. RICE

# Contents

7

# I

# The Pre-Christian Era

Primitive music everywhere, and in all ages, has certain characteristics in common. It is very rhythmic, has simple melodies, is repetitive, and has its origin in the everyday lives of the people—folk music in the purest sense. While acci-

**characteristics**

dental harmonies appear, the basic structure is a unison that may be repeated for hours at a time. The melodic pattern is short, sometimes consisting of only two or three notes. The rhythm, however, may be either monotonously simple or quite complicated, with three or more independent patterns interwoven into bewildering and exciting sounds. The tonal effect is often hypnotic, even to a sophisticated listener.

**earliest musical sounds**

Man probably started using his voice to produce tonal movement of varying degrees of complexity quite early in his development, perhaps even before he learned how to use words. He also discovered that pounding on rocks, wood, skin, and bones produced sounds and rhythms that gave him much satisfaction. Somewhat later he learned how to blow into tubes and across various reeds to produce other interesting sounds, and finally he invented ways of making strings vibrate by plucking them and then by bowing them.

There are three prime sources of information about primitive music:

*sources of information*

1. Archeological studies have provided considerable data.

2. Primitive peoples of today in isolated areas are a living source that is probably dependable. The fact that their tools and implements resemble those of prehistoric man would indicate that similarities exist also in their modes of living.

3. Tradition is a less reliable, but sometimes usable source. For example, various Indian tribes, including those of Mexico and South America, have transmitted literature and music by direct word-of-mouth for many generations.

The taboos, superstitions, spirits, and gods that surround primitive people are so much a part of their lives that it is impossible for them to distinguish between the earthly and

**sacred and secular**

the spiritual. Religion and life are thoroughly intermixed. The same is true of their music. Tonal and rhythmic activities concerned with hunting, fighting, birth, death, and the growth of crops are tied closely to the beliefs that form the basic patterns of their religion. It is doubtful that primitive man has or had any music which could be called strictly secular.

It is almost a certainty that the first music was vocal. Just as a tiny child experiments with sounds, so primitive man explored the effects of varying pitch. His tune may have consisted of two pitches differing by less than a half-step or more than an octave, or it may have been a highly emotional out-

**singing came first**

burst of sound that leapt to great heights, then descended with a ragged movement, only to leap and descend again and again. In the former the effect is that of a chant with emphasis given to words; in the latter words are unimportant because the sounds alone provide emotional release.

*instruments support singing*

Instrumental music first appeared as a supplement to and in support of vocal music. It is important to note that this relationship continued without basic change for thousands of years, until the lute and pipe organ were reasonably well developed in the late fifteenth and early sixteenth centuries.

The Bible contains much information about music in the religious activities of the Jews. Archeological and historical

*Jewish music*

studies of the Egyptians, Assyrians, and Babylonians provide additional usable information, because all the people of the Near East exchanged ideas and customs, including information about the use of instrumental and vocal music. Their religious activities almost invariably depended upon music of some sort. Certain instruments and kinds of songs were designated for specific situations. For example, the Jewish *shofar*, or *ram's horn*, was used primarily as a signaling instrument, while flutes and reed instruments were used to accompany singing.

Most sacred vocal music of the Jews had its origin in secular

*secular influence*

folk songs. Because secular music was associated with dancing and revelry, each song went through a long period of unofficial use before being entirely accepted by the church. This kind of situation has always been, and still is, a factor in the development of sacred music.

Despite its Jewish origin, music of the Western church is

*Greek influence*

more Greek than Jewish. The Greeks established a science of music that was accepted as the foundation upon which the Gregorian modes (scales), as well as musical forms that appeared in succeeding centuries, were constructed.

11

# Early Christian Music

Very early Christian music was remarkable in many ways, not the least being that there was any. The leaders—even as today—were worried by its secular associations. (Instrumental music retained that stigma for centuries and has never been

*early characteristics*

accepted by certain denominations.) Writers of the first two centuries, including Paul, mention the spontaneous outpouring of ecstatic chantlike songs, possibly not unlike the music of primitives, and somewhat similar in origin and purpose to the songs of nineteenth-century American camp meetings. Many Jewish rites, chants, and songs were taken directly into the new church. Antiphonal (two choruses) and responsorial (soloist and congregation) singing of the psalms were adjusted and simplified to suit the demands of Christian worship.

Unlike the Greeks and their Near Eastern neighbors, early Christians were encouraged to consider only the worship

*for worship only*

aspects of music. They believed that beauty as such was too worldly and sensual to have religious value; the ability of music to affect the senses and arouse the emotions was a dangerous asset. Music could be used to draw people away from paganism and into the church, but it could also arouse in them the same thoughts and actions upon which pagan beliefs were founded.

12

## Saint Augustine

Saint Augustine (354-430) was one who expressed deep concern because the effects of music could so easily turn from good to evil. In his *Confessions* (*The Confessions of St. Augustine, Bishop of Hippo*, translated and annotated by J. G. Pilkington [Edinburgh: T. and T. Clark, 1886], pp. 272 ff.) he implied that music is at the mercy of the performer as well as the listener; the same selection can therefore be made to serve secular or sacred purposes. However, the church somewhat reluctantly continued to give vocal music a place of increasing importance because its values to the church were believed to outweigh any negative effects it might have—and it was popular with the people. The Edict of Constantine (313) brought the church out of hiding and, at the same time, enabled music to make a less restrained contribution to worship.

Two items should be emphasized: (1) Church music was thought to have little or no merit except to the extent that it was a part of worship. Its aesthetic value was not to be considered. (2) Church music was congregational and vocal. The former remained true until the early Renaissance, the latter only until the fourth century in the Western church. The Eastern church retained, at least in part, the congregational aspect of its church music. As early as the third century the Western church outlawed the singing of all hymns not found in the Scriptures. This ruling was not especially popular, and from time to time it was ignored by both leaders and laymen.

## Arianism

The struggle over Arianism—out of which came the movement known today as Unitarianism—gave hymn singing a new place of importance during the fourth century. Opposing

13

### early hymns

leaders discovered the propaganda value of hymns. Arius himself, the founder of Arianism, wrote many hymns to popularize his movement after he was condemned by the council of

### Hilary and Ambrose

Nicaea (A.D. 325). Hilary of Poitiers (ca. 310-66) and Ambrose of Milan (ca. 340-ca. 97) were two of his strongest hymn-writing antagonists. At least one hymn by Ambrose, "O splendor of God's glory bright," is in many hymnals today.

### Niceta and Prudentius

Another hymn of the fourth century, the great "Te Deum," is generally credited to a third writer, Niceta of Remesiana (ca. 335-ca. 414). The familiar "Of the Father's love begotten" was written by a Spaniard, Prudentius (348-ca. 413), who was perhaps the best Christian poet of his time.

### the mass

The "official" music of the fourth-century church, that of the mass, was chantlike, derived from Jewish, other Near Eastern, and Greek sources. Its structure was more Greek than anything else, and its language was usually Greek. Until near the time of Gregory the Great, in the sixth and seventh centuries, there was no real church-wide agreement about the structure of the chant or the manner of its use. The church had grown so rapidly that it was a diverse hodgepodge of practices, procedures, and policies. Gregory is often credited with pulling together these diversities and establishing the musical

### Schola Cantorum

and ritualistic patterns of the church. It is strongly possible that more than one pope was involved in this activity, which included the establishment of the Schola Cantorum, a school for the training of church musicians.

14

## Ambrose of Milan

Ambrose of Milan may have been more influential than Gregory in bringing order out of chaos. In addition to his hymn writing, he brought into the Western church musical and ritualistic practices of the Eastern church and attempted to make the chants more consistent in their structure and use. If he and his associates did not actually found the Schola Cantorum they at least started the movement that brought

## Gregory the Great

the school into being. Gregory the Great, late in the sixth century, brought the chants together and clarified them further in his *Antiphonale Missarum* which is still the basic authority on music and worship in the Catholic Church.

## plainsong

The music of Gregorian chant (plainsong) has only one purpose: To aid in the projection of words by creating a smooth flowing line of speech, pleasing to the ear and easily heard. The melodies may be uninteresting and actually boring to modern ears. The chants, however, serve their special purpose better than any other form of church music. After the sixth century Latin was the language of the Western church.

## modes (scales)

It is interesting to note that Gregorian scholars who used the Greek modes as the basis for constructing plainsong melodies mixed up the Greek names. For example, the Greek Dorian became the ecclesiastical Phrygian. The ecclesiastical modes can be identified by playing scales on the white keys of the piano, according to the following patterns:

| | |
|---|---|
| D to D—Dorian | A to A—Hypodorian |
| E to E—Phrygian | B to B—Hypophrygian |
| F to F—Lydian | C to C—Hypolydian |
| G to G—Mixolydian | D to D—Hypomixolydian |

15

The "hypo" modes are a fourth lower than their companions. The church used numbers instead of mode names.

*notation*

Musical notation was almost unknown to pre-Christian peoples. It was certainly inconsistent and not entirely reliable. The earliest Christians developed nothing better. Medieval theorists depended upon a system of notation called *neumes*, signs which merely gave an approximation of melodic movement. During the eleventh century the neumes were placed on one or more lines—the beginning of today's staff—and notation was on its way to becoming an exact science. Guido d'Arezzo invented a system of sightsinging about this time. He suggested as a further aid the use of a familiar hymn whose six phrases start on successive steps of the scale. The first syllable of these phrases were *ut, re, me, fa, sol, la. Ut* later became *do*, and *si* (*ti*) was added to complete the diatonic scale.

*polyphony*

Gregorian chant retained its place as the basic music of the church until the fourteenth and fifteenth centuries when it came into competition with a new style, *polyphony*, which used two or more moving parts (melodic lines) and was

*organum*

divided into measures. Polyphony first appeared about the ninth century as *organum*, a form in which the plainsong is paralleled by an identical melody at an interval of a fourth or fifth below. Addition of octaves increased the voices to three

*counterpoint*

or more. During the next several centuries the plan of changing one or more of the parallel melodies was increasingly accepted until the practice known as *counterpoint* evolved and became the mainstay of composers for centuries. Counterpoint means point (note) against point. The familiar round "Three Blind

16

Mice" is a kind of counterpoint (canon) in which the same melody re-enters one or more times after a lapse of a specified number of beats or measures. Other kinds of counterpoint use two or more melodies which are played or sung together.

### 1. Gregorian chant[1]

Li - be - ra me, Do- mi - ne,

de mor - te ae - ter - na,

### 2. Organum

Sit glo - ri - a Dó - mi - ni;

### 3. Free organum

Cun - cti - po - tens ge - ni - tor de - us,

### 4. Thirteenth century polyphony

Hec

Hec di-

[1] Reprinted by permission of the publishers from Archibald T. Davison and Willi Apel, *Historical Anthology of Music: Oriental, Medieval and Renaissance Music*. Cambridge, Mass.: Harvard University Press, Copyright, 1946, 1949, by The President and Fellows of Harvard College. No. 1, p. 12; no. 2, p. 22; no. 3, p. 22; no. 4, p. 30.

Writers of the medieval period mention the popularity of certain plainsongs; they were often sung by the people in informal situations. Sometimes they were the victims of unfortunate parodies. Secular ideas—musical and otherwise—crept into various masses, and some inevitably gained acceptance. For example, intervals of a fourth, fifth, and an octave were approved for use in the church. A major third was long thought to be sinful because of its association with secular music. Organum was accepted because the "sacred" melody (plainsong) was unchanged even though duplicated. Other kinds of polyphony sometimes were resisted because of the changes this style brought to the plainsong and because polyphony demanded a recurring rhythmic pulse somewhat like that of frowned-upon dances.

### sacred folk music

Sacred folk music was known as early as the seventh century. Many such songs and carols—the latter having originated as "ring" dances—were a mixture of folk language and church Latin or Greek. The familiar "Boar's Head Carol" is a good illustration of this style, which came to be called macaronic:

> The boar's head in hand bear I,
> Bedecked with bay and rosemary;
> And I pray you, my master, be merry,
> Quot estes in convivo:
> Caput apri defero,
> Redens laudes Domino!

### Troubadours

The most famous purveyors of secular music were the Troubadours and Trouveres of France, who had their greatest influence between 1100 and 1300. Their Germanic counterparts, the Minnesingers and Meistersingers, continued to flourish for another century and more. Hans Sachs (1494-

1576) was immortalized by Richard Wagner in his *Die Meistersinger* and is said by some to have been the greatest Meistersinger of them all.

While the Troubadours and their associates were outside the official church, their songs influenced its music. The beauty of colorful music inevitably came into conflict with the beauty of severely simple music (plainsong). The conflict, in one form or another, has continued for centuries.

Developments in organs and organ music have had considerable effect upon church music and worship. Pipe organs

**water organ**

of some sort have been in existence for thousands of years. The *water organ* (*hydralis*), which applied hydraulic principles to obtain constant air pressure, was probably invented during the third century B.C. by Ctesibius of Alexandria. This idea was used in the Near East as late as A.D. 1050.

The pneumatic organ developed in England and France during the eighth century. It was not accepted as a church instrument until the eleventh and twelfth centuries. By 1300 the pipe organ was the basic church instrument.

Early organs—except the small portables—were cumbersome and difficult to play. Keys were as much as five inches

**organ beaters**

wide and were struck with the fists. The performer was called an organ "beater." Ranges were limited and tonal variety was not great. Mechanical improvements during the fourteenth and fifteenth centuries were made necessary by the demands of polyphonic music and, in turn, opened the way for the development of organ techniques not too far removed from those of today. A few organs had as many as three keyboards plus pedal keys. Most of the composers to be discussed in Chap. III were capable organists and composers of organ music.

19

# Reformation and Renaissance

The name of Martin Luther (1483-1546) stands high in

**John Hus**

any discussion of the Reformation. Another great name is often ignored, that of John Hus (ca. 1369-1415), a Bohemian who served as the transition between the English reformer John Wycliffe (ca. 1320-84) and later leaders, including Luther. It was because of his reading the books and promoting the beliefs of Wycliffe that Hus was condemned by the Council of Constance (1414-18) and burned at the stake.

Hus had other heretical tendencies, not the least being his contention that church music should be by as well as for the people. He was himself a singer, and he gave his people many hymns to sing. Some he translated from Latin and some he wrote. It was natural that his followers should become known as a singing church and should publish the first Prot-

**Bohemian Brethren**

estant hymnal (1501). The group was known by this time as the Bohemian Brethren. Many of the Brethren fled to Germany about 1548. Their hymnal had been translated into German in 1531 to accommodate their German-speaking mem-

**Moravians**

bers. Those who remained in Bohemia and Moravia were almost wiped out by later persecutions; about 1725 the entire group moved to Saxony and settled under the protecting arm

20

of a wealthy nobleman, Count Nicolaus Ludwig von Zinzendorf, where they became known as Moravians.

## Herbert, Rinkart, and Gerhardt

Many great hymn writers came out of this little group of consecrated Christians. Their effect upon all of Protestantism would be difficult to measure. Three of the more famous were Peter Herbert (d. 1571, "Now God be with us"); Martin Rinkart (1586-1649, "Now thank we all our God"); Paul Gerhardt (1607-76, "All my heart this night rejoices" and "Jesus, thy boundless love to me"). Johann Crüger (1598-1662) set many Gerhardt texts to music.

## Lutheran hymns

Luther's great contribution to church music was twofold. He wrote and translated hymns and, like Hus, placed great emphasis upon congregational singing. His "A mighty fortress is our God"—both text and tune—alone would have brought him everlasting fame. His followers wrote hundreds of hymns, many of which are still in general use. Some of their tunes were taken from secular sources; others were composed.

## Lutheran composers

Luther was also responsible for encouraging the preparation of much fine choral music by outstanding composers of his time, including Johann Walther (1496-1570) and Ludwig Senfl (ca. 1490-1555). Hans Leo Hassler (1564-1612), Michael Praetorius (1571-1621), and Johann Hermann Schein (1586-1630) made their contributions after Luther's death. These composers wrote polyphonic settings of chorale (hymn) tunes for use by choirs, as well as tunes for the congregation. It was often the practice for congregation and choir to sing alternate stanzas of a chorale, the congregation unaccompained, and in unison, and the choir in parts, accompanied by organ or other instruments. (During the seventeenth century the organ assumed its present-day role of accompanying all Protestant congregational singing. In fact it became too dominant during the eighteenth century and temporarily lost much of its prestige as a result.)

## Calvin

The other great name in Reformation times is that of John Calvin (1509-64). He was personally opposed to the use of any kind of music in the church, but bowed slightly to popular pressure and permitted the unaccompanied singing of biblical texts. Psalms were reconstituted in metrical style, given tunes that were sometimes composed but more often borrowed from popular songs of the day, and sung in church, school, home, and castle. Instruments were not accepted in the church, and only the simplest kind of harmony was permitted. The conflict between beauty and austerity was on again.

## psalters

During the first half of the sixteenth century a number of *psalters* (collections of metrical psalms) were published in France and Switzerland. Clément Marot (ca. 1497-1544) and Théodore Bèza (1519-1605) translated and arranged most of the texts. Louis Bourgeois (ca. 1510-ca. 61), Claude Goudimel (ca. 1505-72), Claude Le Jeune (1528-1600), and Jan Pieterszoon Sweelinck (1562-1621) composed or arranged most of the tunes. Present-day hymnals contain many texts and tunes from this period.

## English Pre-reformation music

English church music prior to the formation of the Church of England in 1534 was little different from that found in Catholic churches on the continent. Two kinds of services— the mass and the *offices of the canonical hours*—utilized music

22

that had changed little since the time of Gregory, despite the influence of secular music. Thousands of hymns had been sorted through and condensed into one large book, the *Breviary*, and all the rites and chants of the mass were available in the *Missal*. Both were in Latin. When Archbishop Thomas Cranmer (1489-1556) anglicized all this material he eliminated hymns, because the people could not read and he had no monks to fill his choir lofts. It is fortunate that these hymns were revived and made available during the nineteenth century. (See Oxford Movement, p. 67.)

## Post-reformation English psalters

When Mary became queen in 1553 she immediately restored the Catholic Church, and families fled to escape persecution. Some went to Germany, but many more went to Switzerland, where they came under the spell of the new psalters. Elizabeth became queen in 1558, and these people

## Sternhold and Hopkins

returned to England, bringing the psalters with them. Numerous English versions were printed. The first (1556) used metrical psalms from a small collection made by Thomas Sternhold (1549) and works of his friend, John Hopkins. More complete editions of Sternhold and Hopkins were published by John Day in 1561 and 1562. The Scottish Psalter of 1564 included psalms from S and H and Genevan Psalters as well as original Scottish versions. The S and H and Scottish Psalters were very popular, appearing in many editions during the next two centuries.

Psalm singing became literally the rage—in homes, on the street, and at parties and dinners, as well as in church. Queen Elizabeth's sarcasm was apparent when she called them "Geneva jiggs." Even the Puritans accepted the psalters, but expressed approval of unison singing only. Parliament actually outlawed the singing of anything except metrical psalms in any church. Despite her sarcasm Queen Elizabeth was herself responsible for the compilation of one of the 326 known psalters.

## Watts

A few brave souls dared to write sacred poetry from time to time, but not until Isaac Watts published his *Hymns and Spiritual Songs* in 1707 was the stranglehold of the psalters substantially loosened.

## counter reformation

The Reformation inevitably brought a counter-reformation as the Catholic Church attempted to regain its lost influences by eliminating abuses and weaknesses that had crept in during the preceding centuries. Music had become strongly secular; popular tunes appeared with little or no disguise in music designed for use on sacred occasions—even as part of the mass. The pipe organ had become a glorious instrument capable of magnificent and sometimes overwhelming effects. Other instruments, especially brass, had found their sometimes noisy and flamboyant way into the service.

## Council of Trent

The Council of Trent (1545-63) attempted to establish rules that would purify the church. Much attention was given to the state of music; the complete elimination of any kind of polyphonic structure was seriously considered. Fortunately a Netherlander, Jacobus de Kerle (ca. 1531-91), was able to soothe the Council with a series of beautiful musical prayers that were an excellent combination of both polyphonic and *homophonic* ideas—the latter being similar to modern hymn-tune harmonizations. The council finally issued a decree calling only for the elimination of anything not in good taste in a house of God.

24

### early composers

Many great composers of sacred and secular music, most of them priests of the Church, had contributed to the enrichment and secularization that the Council of Trent wished to eliminate. Some of the most important were: Guillaume de Machaut (1300-77), French; Francesco Landino (ca. 1325-97), a blind Italian organist; John Dunstable (ca. 1370-1453), English; Guillaume Dufay (ca. 1400-74), Burgundian; Johannes Ockeghem (ca. 1430-ca. 95), Netherlands; Jacob Obrecht (1452-1505), Netherlands; Josquin des Prés (ca. 1450-1521), Netherlands—but, like others of this period, served in France and Italy as well (Martin Luther considered him to be the greatest of all musicians); Jacob Clement (ca. 1510-ca. 56), Netherlands (known also as Jacobus Clemens and Clemens non Papa); Cristóbal de Morales (ca. 1500-53), Spanish.

### motet

During the thirteenth and fourteenth centuries a new kind of sacred music, the motet, evolved out of experiments with rhythmic and harmonic ideas. Other variations developed when composers inserted another tune between the parallel fifths allowed by the Church (organum) and thus obtained the frowned-upon interval of a third. The various parts were sometimes moved to new positions; often the lowest became the highest, thereby creating a sixth. The English were especially fond of thirds and sixths. The top line came to be known as discant. Perfect parallelism was gradually destroyed by the use of contrary motion and by varying the rhythm in different parts. The trend was toward the production of music for music's sake—a move in opposition to the long-held philosophy of the church.

### 1. Thirteenth century motet[1]

### 2. Fourteenth century motet

### 3. Motet, Josquin des Près (ca. 1450-1521)

[1] Reprinted by permission of the publishers from Archibald T. Davison and Willi Apel, *Historical Anthology of Music: Oriental, Medieval and Renaissance Music.* Cambridge, Mass.: Harvard University Press, Copyright, 1946, 1949, by The President and Fellows of Harvard College. No. 1, p. 33; no. 2, p. 61; no. 3, p. 90, from *Worcester Medieval Harmony* and used with the permission of Dom Anselm Hughes.

It is impossible to define the word motet precisely. Generally it is any composition having a sacred text and intended for use in the church. Grove's *Dictionary of Music and Musicians* includes this statement as part of a three-page discussion: "It was essentially an embroidering of a given (not composed) theme of words-and-music by two or three other sets of words-and-music." [2]

This first serious threat to Gregorian chant contained many characteristics of secular music and absorbed others, including some texts that were definitely sacrilegious, as it gradually moved into a position of dominance in the mass and the offices. Musically speaking, the motet was further enriched, about 1450, by the use of several voices instead of solo voices on each part. Choirs were, however, quite small, ranging from eight to thirty singers.

The Council of Trent was dealing with a serious situation when it attempted to purify the music and worship of the

**Palestrina**

Catholic Church. It is indeed fortunate that a musical giant came along to save the day—Giovanni Pierluigi (ca. 1525-94), who is known by the name of his birthplace, the small town of Palestrina. He spent his adult life in Rome, where he composed a great deal of excellent music, much of which is still sung today by Protestant and Catholic alike. He was able to combine the musical devices, methods, and concepts that had evolved during the preceding four centuries with the spirit of purity so desired by the Council. Two other great musicians, Orlando di Lasso (1532-94) and Tomás Vittoria (ca. 1540-1611) contributed mightily to the development of the golden

[2] H. C. Colles, editor (New York: The Macmillan Company, 1941), III, 527.

27

age of choral music. Worship was restored and beauty was retained.

## English musicians

English musicians of the sixteenth and seventeenth centuries established a standard of choral music unsurpassed elsewhere, and not equalled by later Englishmen until the twentieth century. The greatest among the many were John Taverner (ca. 1495-1545), Christopher Tye (ca. 1500-ca. 72), Thomas Tallis (ca. 1505-85), and Robert White (ca. 1530-74). Tye, Tallis, and White wrote for both Roman and Anglican churches.

The next generation of English composers was more famous for secular than sacred music. Their contributions to the sacred music repertoire, however, were extensive and valuable. Two men deserve special mention: William Byrd (1543-1623) and Orlando Gibbons (1583-1625). Byrd composed both secular and sacred music; Gibbons wrote principally for the church. The deaths of these two men and the ascendancy of the Puritans in 1649 put an end to English leadership in music, and particularly church music.

## of vocal and instrumental music

Vocal music reached a climax in Europe during the sixteenth century; instrumental music merely continued its slow progress. The lute had attained status as an independent performer of secular music; the organ served a comparable purpose in the church. Both continued to accompany vocal music. While the lute soon passed its peak of popularity and began a downward plunge, the organ was reaching for the first of its many high points. By the late 1500's organists had developed a large repertoire of preludes, incidental music, and even portions of the mass that had previously been sung.

28

### Venetian composers

Venice—especially the Cathedral of Saint Mark—was a major center of Italian church music during the climactic sixteenth century. The first Venetian composers and conduc-

### Willaert

tors of this period were originally from the Netherlands. Adrian Willaert (ca. 1490-1562) was one of the most famous.

### Gabrielis

Later the Italians took over, the two most famous being Andrea Gabrieli (ca. 1510-86) and his nephew Giovanni Gabrieli (ca. 1557-1612). Music written especially for and performed in Saint Mark's Cathedral employed brass and stringed instruments as well as organs. Giovanni Gabrieli sometimes used five choruses in a single composition, each chorus utilizing various combinations of voices and instruments. The effect of this kind of music, performed in the proper setting, was and is magnificent beyond description. It is interesting to observe that most successful musicians of the sixteenth and seventeenth centuries, including those who wrote for Lutheran churches, spent some time in study at Saint Mark's, or studied with someone who had.

The beauty of holiness and the holiness of beauty were brought close together for a brief period of time; the baroque era was just about ready to blossom forth.

29

# The Baroque Era

The term *baroque* was originally one of derision, implying a degeneration. (Modern fresh-water pearls which are irregular in shape and size are called baroque pearls.) Actually the

**Baroque—definition**

period—roughly 1600-1750—was one of experimenting with new interpretations of old rules and regulations and of seeking for new truths. It concerned all the arts, including literature; its attitude of inquiry was felt even in the sciences. Musicians found it necessary to master the old (*stile antico*) before venturing into the new (*stile moderno*). Many composers moved freely from one style to the other, utilizing the best of each for particular situations.

One of the most significant products of the new style was an increased emphasis upon solo singing, patterned to a certain extent after the ancient Greek recitation. The form was

**characteristics**

called monody (*monodia: monos*, alone; *aidein*, to sing). True monody was a kind of song-speech with a very sketchy accompaniment. The first opera—ca. 1594—was primarily monodic in structure, consisting almost entirely of dramatic recitations (*recitatives*).

**cantata**

The Roman church was quick to recognize the teaching as well as musical value of this medium and developed the cantata, a short dramatic solo which might tell a story, narrate a sacred poem, or present a passage of scripture. In its earliest form the Italian cantata consisted entirely of short, contrasting sections. After 1650 it became much longer—up to fifteen minutes in length—and included several alternating recitatives and arias (solos with moving melodic lines). More often than not it was entirely secular; sacred words were sometimes used, however.

## Lutheran cantata

The Lutheran cantata appeared about 1700; it was a musical setting of poetry which managed to please conservative and liberal churchmen alike by alternating prescribed hymns or passages of scripture with original sacred poetry. Music for the latter was inclined to be rather florid and operatic in character. Certain portions consisted of recitatives and arias, and others of choral ensembles. Johann Sebastian Bach (1685-1750) is the most famous of all composers utilizing this form. His cantatas employ solo and ensemble voices and instruments in masterful and varied combinations. He is said to have composed three hundred sacred cantatas during his very busy lifetime.

Another kind of dramatic presentation appeared about 1600—a stage performance differing from opera only in that
## oratorio
its text was sacred. It was really an oversized morality play with music, and although not particularly successful, certain of its characteristics were retained when it was completely reconstructed to fit the needs of the church. Acting and staging were eliminated, leaving only the dramatic effects obtainable by solo and chorus with accompanying instruments. The form came to be called oratorio, from the little room or chapel called the oratory in which a Jesuit priest, Fillipo de' Neri

(1515-95), first presented the simple yet dramatic musical prayer service that seemed to fill a great need in the lives of his people. About 1555 a society grew out of these prayer-song meetings; it took the name *Congregazione dell' Oratorio*. When the attempt to compete with opera failed, church musicians returned to the ideas of Neri for the development of a form more consistent with current attitudes toward church music.

The oratorio of the seventeenth century differed little from opera except in its lack of acting and staging. Solos ran the gamut from accompanied or unaccompanied recitatives to extremely colorful, even florid, arias. Choruses were full and exciting or quiet and prayerful as the text demanded. Accompanying instruments were used to support and strengthen the entire presentation. Giacomo Carissimi (ca. 1604-74) was the most successful Italian oratorio composer of the period. The

**Schütz, Bach, and Handel**

greatest, however, were Germans. Next to J. S. Bach and George Frederick Handel (1685-1759), and preceding them by a century, was Heinrich Schütz (1585-1672), who was equally proficient in other vocal forms. Two of his oratorios—*The Seven Last Words* and *The Christmas Oratorio*—are sung frequently today.

No study of oratorio is complete without some discussion of Handel. His *Messiah* alone assures him of lasting fame. Handel's oratorios were written for English audiences and were generally based on passages of scripture, selected by a librettist according to the manner in which the composer wished to tell his story. He used recitative, aria, chorus, and orchestra to construct monumental works whose greatness was immediately apparent and whose influence upon eighteenth and nineteenth century English church music was profound.

*passions*

The oratorios of Bach bear a special name, *passions;* they are all concerned with Christ's suffering and death. While Handel identifies no individuals in his *Messiah,* Bach calls upon the persons concerned with the events to speak in recitative and aria. Christ, Barabbas, Pilate, and others come to life. A narrator is used to relate events as they occur, and the chorus sometimes portrays a raging crowd, sometimes a sorrowing world, and sometimes a deeply concerned yet somewhat impersonal philosopher. This style of sacred choral writing had actually been used in one form or another as early as the thirteenth century. The first composer to make adaptations for Protestant use was Johann Walther, whose *St. Matthew Passion* appeared about 1550. Heinrich Schütz's *Seven Last Words* was perhaps the first *oratorio-passion.* Bach seems to have been influenced greatly by this work. Handel's setting of the Passion according to Saint John, written when the composer was eighteen years of age, was probably the result of his study of Schütz.

*Haydn*

Franz Joseph Haydn (1732-1809) left two ambitious choral works that are somewhat similar to Handel's oratorios. *The Seasons* and *The Creation* combine scripture and poetry in a manner that seems closer to the so-called romantic nineteenth-century era than to his period, the classic eighteenth century.

Since the time of J. S. Bach and Handel the terms oratorio and cantata have been bandied carelessly about until they have little or no meaning. Almost any sacred choral work that includes solos and choruses with instrumental accompaniment may be called an oratorio if it is quite involved and/or long, or a cantata if it is somewhat less complicated and/or relatively short.

Mention should be made of the unique liturgical-musical

form, the English *anthem*, which appeared early in the seven-
*anthem composers*

teenth century. Unlike the metrical psalms, and differing somewhat in structure from the sixteenth-century Latin motet,
anthems were choir settings of scripture and prayers. John
Blow (ca. 1649-1708), Henry Purcell (ca. 1659-95), Pelham
Humphrey (1647-74), and William Croft (1678-1727) were
the most famous members of a very large group of composers
whose anthems and *services* were the mainstay of English
sacred choral music. Some anthems included solos and
choruses, some only choruses. Many of the latter type are in
the repertoire of today's choirs.

*the service*

The service, which preceded the anthem and prepared the
way for its development, had its origin in the English antipathy
toward anything Roman. Composers were encouraged to write
music for certain of the old offices, especially those to be sung
in the early morning and evening, and a complete musical
service resulted. In 1560 John Day published what is generally
considered to be the first significant collection of music designed specifically for the new church. The title is indicative
of its purpose: *Certaine Notes Set Forth in Foure and Three
Parts to be Sung at the Morning Communion, and the Evening Praier.*

Very little instrumental music of any real consequence
other than organ music has been written for use in Protestant
churches since the time of Bach. The Gabrielis in Venice
composed sacred music for various instrumental ensembles as
did also Arcangelo Corelli (1653-1713) and Giuseppi Torelli
(1658-1709). The perfecting of the violin in the seventeenth
century turned the emphasis toward stringed instruments—
solo and ensembles—and orchestras. From this time on instru-

mental groups became primarily purveyors of secular music and the field of sacred instrumental music was left almost entirely to the organ.

### baroque organ

The seventeenth-century (baroque) organ in Germany and Italy was tonally and mechanically an excellent instrument. In Italy the leading organist-composer was Girolamo Frescobaldi (1583-1643). Two of his pupils were the great Germans Dietrich Buxtehude (1637-1707) and Johan Pachelbel (1653-1706). Bach walked two hundred miles in order to hear Buxtehude play. He was greatly influenced by both of these pupils of Frescobaldi and by mechanical improvements made during the sixteenth and early seventeenth centuries, including the development of a more playable pedal board. (His music, and the music of his immediate predecessors, is usually a part of the twentieth-century organist's repertoire.) The organist's technique, not the limitations of the instrument, became the determining factor in performance.

Organs and organists outside Germany lagged far behind. Instruments constructed as late as 1700 rarely had pedal boards, and their overall construction was not conducive to effective performance. Even the Italians failed to continue the advances made by Frescobaldi.

Baroque organists composed and performed in many forms
### organ music
and styles. One of the earliest was called *ricercar*, which was a kind of counterpoint that had in it the seeds of the *fugue*. Ricercar comes from a word meaning "to search out," a meaning which is apparent in the intermingling of moving melodic lines. The *fantasia* was a free style that could follow any one of many forms, but usually was intended to sound like an improvisation. The *toccata* (root word, *tocare*, mean-

ing "to beat") was the form most used by baroque organists to display their virtuosity, especially with the pedals. It was often a show piece, full of color, contrast, and excitement and followed no specified form. Buxtehude's toccatas were better disciplined in structure than those of other composers, even to the extent of incorporating some strict counterpoint in the middle section.

## choral prelude

Lutheran organists of the seventeenth century depended heavily on the *choral prelude*, which was originally what its name implies—a prelude to congregational singing of a chorale. The preludes became increasingly colorful and lengthy until they were actually independent organ solos. Four, and possibly five, different forms of the prelude evolved:

1. "Pure" choral prelude, in which the melody is played in long notes against moving accompaniment.

2. Choral *fughetta*, in which each movement or section is in the form of a little fugue.

3. Choral *fantasia*, which is as its name suggests—a free improvisation on a chorale.

4. Choral *partita*, which is a set of variations on a chorale. The fifth, untitled group, is well represented by the familiar "Jesu, joy of man's desiring."

## the fugue

A sophisticated kind of counterpoint—the fugue—was an outgrowth of the old ricercar. The root word means "to flee" and aptly describes the fugue. A round, such as "Three Blind Mice," has some of the characteristics of a fugue. The same tune is repeated two or more times after the lapse of a specified number of beats. In a true fugue the tune is usually repeated in a related key and may or may not be altered slightly. The greatest master of this style of composition was J. S. Bach.

His fugues are an almost unbelievable interweaving of the tune or tunes.

Whether the listener is affected favorably or unfavorably by baroque music, the period cannot be ignored. A time of experimentation and exuberant adolescence was necessary before music could move beyond the limitations established by the rules and regulations that had evolved during the preceding centuries.

# V

# The Eighteenth Century in Europe

*secular dominance*

The study of music prior to the sixteenth century is primarily the study of church music. Since the close of the sixteenth century the church has become increasingly more unimportant in the overall musical picture. J. S. Bach was one of the last great musicians whose life was devoted especially to the composing and performing of sacred music which was designed primarily to fulfill the needs of a worship service. While Handel was and is famous for his sacred oratorios, it is also true that he wrote large quantities of secular instrumental and vocal music, including many operas and a few oratorios.

*congregational music*

Protestant leaders have from the beginning of the Reformation given emphasis to congregational music, whether it be the hymns of Hus, the chorales of Luther, or the metrical psalms of Calvin. Much of the remainder of this study will be concerned with developments related to hymnody. Consideration will be given to music for organ and choir as significant events occur, but those events will be found to occur less frequently than in earlier times.

*Watts*

Isaac Watts (1674-1748) is credited with opening the hearts and minds of English-speaking churchmen to the value of sacred poetry that is not necessarily a version of the scriptures. As with leaders in other periods and in other areas of knowledge, his contributions were made possible by the work of less famous men of preceding generations.

### earliest English hymn writers

George Herbert (1593-1633) was an Anglican priest who wrote sacred poetry for himself and his friends, who published his collection *The Temple: or Sacred Poems and Private Ejaculations* in 1633. One of his best-known hymns is "Teach me, my God and King." The fame of John Milton (1608-74) rests upon his great "Paradise Lost." He was equally adept at writing sacred poems, however, most of which were versions of the Psalms. A good example is "Let us with a gladsome mind," which Milton adapted from Ps. 136 when he was only fifteen years old. Thomas Ken (1637-1711) wrote two famous poems for the boys of his school, Winchester College: "Awake, my soul, and with the sun," and "All praise to thee, my God, this night" for use as morning and evening hymns. The final stanza of each is the well-known Doxology, "Praise God from whom all blessings flow."

### Watts—background

Isaac Watts seems to have had everything against him, except faith and perseverance. He was more than homely—he was ugly; his health was poor; he was quite unlucky in love; and he was so precocious that he found himself often out of touch with his generation. He wrote acceptable poetry when he was a small child. His first hymn was written because he was irritated by the singing in his church, and his father challenged him to write something better—actually no challenge for this fifteen-year-old genius. During his lifetime he poured out a constant stream of sacred poetry. His first published collection—*Hymns and Spiritual Songs* (1707)—was intended to "furnish hymns for the meanest of Christians."

This collection, like his other writings, was extremely popular because he wrote simply and plainly in a style that anyone could understand. A good illustration is the familiar "When I survey the wondrous cross."

## the Wesleys

Many English poets attempted to imitate Watts; some succeeded, but many failed. A contemporary, Charles Wesley (1707-88), is often called the greatest hymn writer of all times. Actually, it is doubtful that he or his brother John (1703-91) consciously imitated anyone or anything. They did, however, acknowledge the debt the church owed to Watts. Little need be said about the contribution to congregational singing made by the Wesleys—Charles, the writer of probably eight thousand hymns, and John, the painstaking translator and editor.

## Wesley and the Moravians

Some of John Wesley's most effective work is found in his translations of Moravian hymns. Wesley traveled to the American colonies with a shipload of Moravians, who impressed him with their effective use of hymns in times of deep distress. He improved his understanding of the German lan-

## the first Wesley hymnal

guage for the express purpose of learning their hymns. This experience, plus the inadequacy of the Authorized Psalter, led him to compile the first collection of hymns for practical use in public worship by Anglican congregations, A Collection of Psalms and Hymns. Charles Town, 1737. He was especially interested in the writings of Paul Gerhardt, Gerhard Tersteegen (1697-1769, "Thou hidden love of God"), and Nicolas Zinzendorf (1700-60, "O Thou, to whose all-searching sight"). The last named will be remembered as the sponsor and protector of the followers of John Hus, who fled from Bohemia and

Moravia. Zinzendorf was a landed nobleman who put his wealth where his heart and soul led him to place it. He became not only the protector of the Moravians but their leader as well. He wrote many fine hymns during his lifetime of service.

## German hymn writers

There were other German hymn writers of the period from 1650 to 1800 in addition to those mentioned on page 21 whose influence is still felt. Three should be at least mentioned: Friedrich von Canitz (1654-99, "Come, my soul, thou must be waking"); Joachim Neander (1650-80, "Praise to the Lord, the Almighty"), who wrote tunes for many of his hymns; and Matthias Claudius (1740-1815, "We plow the fields and scatter").

The successful use of hymns in congregational singing and private devotion by the Wesleys led many others to enter the field, often for the expressed purpose of proving a point in theology or of leading unbelievers to a different way of life—even if it meant leaving one church in order to form or join another. Some of the more famous were William Williams (1717-91, "Guide me, O Thou great Jehovah"); Augustus Toplady (1740-78, "Rock of Ages"); John Newton, a man of many lives including that of a slave-ship captain (1725-1807, "Glorious things of thee are spoken"); William Cowper, who collaborated with Newton in the preparation and publication of the *Olney Hymns* (1731-1800, "God moves in a mysterious way").

These men, like the Wesleys, all had their roots in the established church. Some, like Williams, moved far from the church of their youth; others, like Newton, kept the ties unbroken.

## hymn tunes

English hymn tunes of the late seventeenth and much of the eighteenth centuries were many times written to please and sometimes were even borrowed from current popular songs. The number of tunes from this period that are in use today is extremely small, even though the need to express the unusual hymn-text meters of Wesley and other evangelical hymns still exists. Representative of the best are "Hanover" and "St. Anne," by William Croft; "Darwell," by John Darwell (1731-89). Even those Handel composed for the Wesleys are no longer sung; only a few tunes that were arranged or adapted from Handel's music are in common use today. The florid, somewhat vapid melodies generally written for hymns had only a transitory appeal.

Wesley's *Foundery Collection*, a hymn-tune book published in 1742, was remarkable for the quality of its tunes. Of those in use today, "Savannah," "Easter Hymn," and "Amsterdam" are representative examples. Wesley often wrote of his displeasure over the trend toward less effective congregational music. His tracts on church music are interesting reading and still surprisingly applicable. He did not completely approve of *Harmonia Sacra*, a collection which his good friend Thomas Butts published in 1753. He, therefore, prepared a book that he hoped would serve all the needs of his people and issued it in 1761 as *Select Hymns with Tunes Annext*. The tune section was entitled *Sacred Melody*. A corrected and enlarged edition was published in 1765 and reprinted in 1770. Wesley disguised his sponsorship of a third tune book by publishing it anonymously in 1781. Its complete title is indicative of trends in Methodist singing: *Sacred Harmony, or a choice Collection of Psalm and Hymn Tunes In two or three parts For the Voice, Harpsichord, and Organ.*

psalm singing

It must be remembered that congregational singing in the Church of England was "officially" limited to the Psalms until 1821. Hymn tunes were, therefore, produced by those who were concerned with the needs of the Wesleyan and other evangelical groups. Even so great a source of tunes as the *Collection of Psalm Tunes* of Isaac Smith (ca. 1770) was affected by this trend. In the words of Erik Routley, ". . . we find alongside these powerful and gracious eighteenth century tunes a whole series of tunes in the Wesleyan idiom." [1] The first Baptist tune book, John Rippon's publication of 1796, offers a survey of late eighteenth-century popular tunes, being a somewhat representative sampling of other collections of the time, including a number of tunes by Handel and his imitators.

### Scottish psalmody

A shining light of stubborn conservatism existed in Scotland through the seventeenth century; only five psalm tunes were considered permissible. After 1775 there was a slight relaxation of restrictions, but the effects of this relaxation were inconsequential.

The great musicians of the eighteenth century, beyond those already mentioned, had little to do with church music.

### Bach

J. S. Bach's large choral works, other than the Passions, were somewhat limited in number but do include his *Magnificat*

### Mozart

and *Mass in B Minor*. Wolfgang Amadeus Mozart (1756-91) contributed a number of concert masses, several motets, and seventeen "epistle sonatas" for organ and orchestra.

It should be noted that almost all music written prior to the early nineteenth century was either commissioned for a special event or composed as part of the musician's regular

---

[1] *The Music of Christian Hymnody* (London: Independent Press Ltd., 1957), p. 98.

job, the latter made necessary by the lack of printed music. Bach wrote his three hundred cantatas for immediate use.

## gebrauchmusik

Professional musicians were often hard pressed to meet day-to-day and week-to-week demands. As a general rule, individual selections were repeated two or three times and then put away indefinitely. It is no wonder that little attention was given to such a mundane matter as the writing of hymn tunes.

## Beethoven

The greatest musician of the late eighteenth and early nineteenth centuries was Ludwig van Beethoven (1770-1827). He was no more concerned with sacred music than were his peers, despite his being a devout person whose beliefs seem to have been tinged with mysticism. His *Mass in D* (*Missa Solemnis*) is his one great sacred work. Unlike the masses of Bach and Mozart which consist of several independent sections, the *Mass in D* is a choral symphony whose movements correspond to the five major sections of the *ordinary of the mass*. As with all of Beethoven's compositions, it is logically constructed with every part contributing to a unified whole.

## Hymn to joy

While Beethoven wrote no hymn tunes as such, one of the greatest hymn tunes of all time—"Hymn to joy"—is derived, almost literally, from the last movement of his *Ninth* (Choral) *Symphony*. (The most familiar words are "Joyful, joyful, we adore Thee," written by Henry van Dyke [1852-1933] about 1910 just for this tune.) Beethoven's one oratorio, *Christ on the Mount of Olives*, contains some excellent choral music but is rarely performed in its entirety.

It must not be assumed that there was a shortage of hymn tunes. On the contrary, the problem was one of quantity with-

## German tune composers

out quality. Of the dozens—perhaps hundreds—of German tune composers the following are probably the best: C. F. Witt (ca. 1660-1716) whose *Psalmodia Sacra* (1715) was a standard collection of better-than-average quality ("Stuttgart" is a good example); J. C. Kuhnau (1735-1805); Christian Gregor (1723-1801), a Moravian. With the exception of Witt, these men were undoubtedly led astray by the seductive melodies of secular German music whose appeal was instantaneous and transitory. It is fortunate that later German composers of hymn tunes returned to a more solid style despite the romantic influence of the nineteenth century.

## English and continental choirs

Many large churches in England and on the continent have a long history of choirs, some of excellent caliber. Martin Luther encouraged the development of congregational singing, but he and his followers also recognized the contribution that a well-trained choir could make to worship. By 1700 it was the accepted procedure that portions of the service be given to a choir—if the church could maintain one. Certain dissenter groups were opposed to this practice and to the use of instruments, but the Lutheran and Anglican churches actively supported their choirs. Organists and/or choirmasters were encouraged to develop the best possible music program. Cathedrals maintained choir schools out of which came their all-male choirs—boy sopranos and altos, adult tenors and basses.

Despite the popularity of choirs, English choral music of the eighteenth century was generally less than ordinary. Pur-

## Purcell

cell was the climactic figure of English Post-reformation sacred music. His death in 1695 left a void that remained long *poor quality*

unfilled. Italian opera inevitably made its influence felt in England, where Handel and others ground out those stylized, florid, musical collections of tinsel and tapestry that were extremely popular during the first half of the century. A few church musicians resisted, but even their music was affected. Maurice Greene (1695-1755), William Boyce (1710-79), and Samuel Wesley (1766-1837) retained some of Purcell's purity and stability. It is interesting to note that Wesley was the son of hymn writer Charles Wesley. Samuel was the greatest English organist of his generation.

*Boyce*

William Boyce is famous for his three volume collection *Cathedral Music*, published in 1760, 1768, and 1778. It is a monumental work, but today's musicologist is amazed by the "corrections" he inserted in music of the Elizabethan period. The corrections are usually errors. Boyce and his associates were totally ignorant of the stylistic demands of the barless music of Tallis and Gibbons. The benefits that might have accrued to eighteenth-century composers from studying the works of their now famous predecessors were lost.

Many small churches had no organ; others had no trained musician to lead them. Printed music was extremely scarce. Various combinations of instruments, usually determined by what was available, were often used to accompany the congre-

*the barrel organ*

gation and any other singers. The *barrel organ*, a mechanical instrument which applied the music-box principle, was quite popular toward the end of the century, primarily because of the lack of organists. Under the circumstances it is safe to assume that music during the eighteenth century was more often a liability than an asset in many English churches.

46

*continental organ music*

When competent musicians and adequate organs were available, as in many continental churches—especially in Germany—the organ music was often of excellent quality. The eighteenth-century organ was designed to display chorale tunes and similar thematic material in various contrapuntal forms. The concept was one of flowing, horizontal lines, so transparent in texture that no one part remained dominant, unless it was intended to be heard as a solo. There are those who maintain, and with considerable justification, that much organ music of the classic period is equal to any choral or instrumental music of any other period and superior to most in terms of quality and worship characteristics.

# VI

# America, 1600–1800

There is little doubt that every New-World colony had
**earliest New World music**
some sort of music for the church and the home. Records are
available which mention the music used in 1494 in Santa Do-
mingo. Other Spanish-American settlements showed interest
in music, even to the extent of publishing the first American
book containing music, *Ordinarium*, printed in Mexico City
in 1556. About 1600 the Mission of San Felipe, New Mexico,
was the scene of considerable musical activity.

Colonies of traders existed on the New England coast before the Pilgrims landed in 1620. The Huguenots who settled
temporarily in Carolina in 1572 had their collections of metri-
**Pilgrims**
cal psalms. The Pilgrims, however, were the first to remain
and to leave a record of their musical practices. They brought
with them the *Book of Psalmes* (1612) prepared by Henry
Ainsworth for the Separatists who first went to Holland.

**Puritans**
Music—especially singing—played a vital role in the lives
of the Pilgrims and their neighbors, the Massachusetts Bay
Puritans, who sang from Sternhold and Hopkins *The Whole
Booke of Psalmes*, which was based on the *Genevan Psalter of
1562*. Each of these collections contains a number of interesting and effective tunes.

Musicologists are generally agreed that the early colonists not only delighted in their singing but sang quite well. Writers of the seventeenth century mention the presence of fine

**colonial psalm singing**

musicians during the early years. It is certain that they sang with vigor and had little patience with lethargic, mournful music. The Ravenscroft (1621) collection of 105 tunes was very popular among the Puritans. Some of the arrangements are of sufficiently high calibre to challenge a good twentieth-century choir—and they were intended for home and congregational use.

The varied meters and difficult melodic, harmonic, and rhythmic structure of the tunes and psalms brought from England proved too difficult for the next generation. In 1640 the

**Bay Psalm Book**

colonists published *The Whole Booke of Psalmes*, commonly known as *The Bay Psalm Book*, in which the psalms were set in simple meter, usually common (8.6.8.6). This first colonial effort at publication of any kind of book was crude, lacking literary style and consistent form. It became extremely popular in the colonies, however, and strangely enough, was used by some congregations in England. The ninth edition (1698) was the first to include tunes—thirteen in number.

**precentor**

The practice of depending upon the precentor, or song-leader, to "line out" the Psalms was followed until about 1800, and to a certain extent, another fifty years in various parts of the country where music training was deficient or lacking. The precentor read, sang, or chanted one phrase at a time and was echoed by the congregation in somewhat the following manner:

Precentor: "The Lord to mee a Shepheard is,"

49

> Congregation: "The Lord to mee a Shepheard is,"
> Precentor: "want therefore shall not I."
> Congregation: "want therefore shall not I."

Since trained precentors were few, and each one was inclined to add his own peculiar interpretations to the tunes, singing degenerated into a kind of provincial folk music that could hardly be identified with its origins. Individual members of the congregation often felt the need to express themselves with variations upon the precentor's variations. Confusion of a rather exciting kind was the result.

Educated churchmen recognized the need for reform early in the eighteenth century. The Reverend John Tufts (1689-1750) published a twelve-page pamphlet, *A very plain and easy introduction to the whole Art of Singing Psalm Tunes,*

**fasola system**

possibly as early as 1721. He attempted to introduce the so-called *fasola* method of sightsinging in which a diatonic scale in any key would be read *fa, so, la, fa, so, la, mi* (equivalent to *do, re, mi, fa, sol, la, ti*). A system of punctuation marks designated time values. The pamphlet was of some significance, being the first such attempt. Tufts' system did not revolutionize the singing of his day, however.

**the "new way" versus the "old way"**

Other ministers followed Tufts' lead. Thomas Symmes (1677-1725), Thomas Walter (1696-1725), and the famous Cotton Mather (1662-1728) wrote and preached in favor of the "new way"—singing with notes—as opposed to the "old way"—folk singing with no rules or notes. The tendency to add embellishments of varying complexity and duration had become so pronounced that the original tune was often difficult to find. Walter's book *The Grounds and Rules of Musick Explained* (Boston: J. Franklin, 1721) was his attempt to restore some order to singing. In his preface he speaks of the "twistings of the old way" and the tunes that were "miserably tortured, and twisted, and quavered" beyond recognition.

The bitterness engendered by efforts to restore congregational singing to its original excellent status is difficult to be-

*style of singing*

lieve. The "old" way had apparently become a part of the people's lives; "lining out" seems hardly to have been necessary because the tunes were few—most congregations sang only four or five—and the psalms had certainly been memorized by everyone. Apparently the people did not wish to give up the slow, drawling style of singing. Gilbert Chase describes the singing quite graphically.

... the singing is very slow; many grace notes, passing notes, turns, flourishes and other ornaments are used; pitch and time values are arbitrarily altered; there is a lack of synchronization among the voices; everyone sings as best pleases himself.[1]

Precentors were not a colonial invention. Actually, their use was recommended in English churches by the Westminster assembly of 1645. The Scottish church resisted the suggestion for some time, but finally accepted it so completely that the custom continued until after 1800 despite attempts by the church to abolish it. The same reluctance was encountered in America; hearts were bruised as choirs took over the leadership of congregational singing.

*singing schools*

The need for better music in the churches led to the establishment of "singing schools" in homes, churches, and "meeting houses." Simple rudiments were taught, and an effort was

---

[1] *America's Music* (New York: McGraw-Hill Book Company, 1955), p. 30.

made to popularize a more unified kind of singing. Such schools were not unknown in the early seventeenth century, but seem to have languished until about 1720, when they were revived and given added importance by ministers and laymen alike. Isaac Watts and his concern for congregational music other than metrical psalms created more problems because the dispute had been previously concerned only with psalm singing.

### development of choirs

The gradual development of choirs was an added factor. By the middle of the century many of the larger city churches had separated their "leading" singers from the congregation, usually placing them in the balcony. The choirs were not long in expecting special consideration. In the minds of these "important" singers metrical psalms were not sufficiently challenging. They demanded, and ultimately received, "special" music, about which more will be said later.

### first American hymn writer

Timothy Dwight (1752-1817), an American Congregationalist, was the first American hymn writer to accept Watts' attitude completely. He was asked in 1791 to revise an American edition of Watts' *Psalms and Hymns* made earlier by Joel Barlow. He included thirty-three of his own hymns, of which only "I love Thy kingdom, Lord" is in use today. Dwight lived a full and influential life, climaxed by his serving as president of Yale.

Various denominations, often assigned the inclusive term "Dissenters," had considerable effect upon eighteenth-century

### Shakers

American music. The Shakers, who came to New York State from England in 1774, were greatly interested in music of a

**Mennonites**

more exciting kind than psalm singing. The earliest Mennonites brought their hymnal of 1583 (*Der Ausbund*) to Pennsyl-

**Pietists**

vania during the late 1600's. The Pietists, another group that
accepted Quaker hospitality (1694), were lead by Johannes
Kelpius, an amateur musician of sorts. In 1703 the Pietists'
musical skills were displayed in a service—perhaps the ordina-
tion of Justus Falckner as pastor—in Old Swedes Church
(Gloria Dei), which still stands in Philadelphia. They used
string, woodwind, brass, and percussion instruments and a
small organ. Being asked to present this service was no small
honor since the Swedish Lutherans, who founded the church
in 1700, had brought from Sweden the traditions of fine singing of fine music.

Kelpius and his translator, Christopher Witt, formerly of
England, prepared a collection of hymns and tunes in 1705.
The tunes are not considered to be original compositions,

**organs**

being instead "borrowed" from various German sources. It is
interesting to note that, among other activities, Witt probably
built the first American organ. Early Americans were somewhat slow to accept the organ as a church instrument; un-
availability of good organs was probably a big reason for the
slowness. A number of excellent church organs were in existence in America by the end of the eighteenth century. Church
organs of recital calibre came along later, there being only a
few by 1850.

**Ephrata Cloister**

Members of Ephrata (Pennsylvania) Cloister, which was
established in 1720 as an offshoot of the Mennonites, had a
great influence on early American culture—far out of propor-

tion to their numbers, which never exceeded three hundred. They included printers, composers, singers, teachers. Franklin, Washington, Francis Hopkinson (1737-91) and other leaders of the day attended their school.

Ephrata singing was probably unaccompanied. The voices were divided into four to seven parts and the effect was undoubtedly startling to ears accustomed to undisciplined psalm singing. The Ephrata musicians were undisciplined in a different sense—they composed and sang according to their own rules, which gave little heed to conventionalities. Their leader, Conrad Beissel, was something of a musical dictator, even to the establishing of rules for composition in his *Dissertation on Harmony*. Benjamin Franklin printed several of their hymnbooks. The title of the most comprehensive collection—of some 750 hymns—is interesting: *Song of the Lonely and Forsaken Turtle Dove, the Christian Church*. This was usually abbreviated to *Turtel-Taube*.

## Moravians

The Moravians, who started with John Hus in the fifteenth century, were still a compact group of dedicated Christians when they came to Georgia in 1735. By 1740 most of the group had removed to Bethlehem, Pennsylvania, where they became a dominant factor in the cultural and economic life of Pennsylvania. Their Collegium Musicum was a musical society that presented great music of the day—Haydn, Mozart, C. P. E. Bach, and Handel. It is quite likely that their *Messiah* was the first New-World performance of that work. When part of the group moved to Winston-Salem, North Carolina, they carried their influence with them. Many of the churches they built are still standing, and every church had its own organ.

The Moravians were competent, even excellent, musicians.

54

They were at home with instrumental and vocal ensembles as composers, performers, and listeners. Their compositions for

*Peter*

trombone are especially exciting. The string quintets of Johann Friedrich Peter (1746-1813) are of sufficiently high calibre to be used on the same program with Mozart and Haydn. The latter's influence upon Peter is quite noticeable. Peter was, among other things, organist for his church.

Two interesting facets of Moravian life deserve special attention—their concern for missionary work and their interest in all peoples everywhere. They prepared hymnals in native Indian languages—the first for the Delawares in 1763; they sponsored an international "sing," September 4, 1745, in Bethlehem, at which a hymn was sung in thirteen languages simultaneously.

### Protestant Episcopal Church

The Protestant Episcopal Church in early America differed little from its English counterpart in the attention given to music, following the same practices in regard to singing metrical psalms and depending upon the same music for Morning and Evening Prayer—the two services most commonly used. The larger churches had small gallery (balcony) choirs; at least three probably had boy choirs. Trinity Church, New York, may have started a sort of singing school in connection with the founding of its charity boys' school in 1709. Their singing

*boy choirs*

is mentioned in the church minutes of 1739. Christ Church, Philadelphia, employed Francis Hopkinson in 1764 to teach music to the children. St. Michael's, Charleston, South Carolina, formed a trained boy choir from children in the city orphanage about 1792 and for some time maintained an outstanding program of church music. The rules set up to govern

55

the activities and responsibilities of the organist and others connected with the music are quite detailed and make interesting reading.[2]

## European influence

Mention should be made of European-born American musicians whose influence was most pronounced during the seventeenth century. The first of any consequence was Carl Pachelbel (1690-1750), son of the organist whom Bach so admired, and himself an accomplished organist. His extended visit to the colonies lasted from 1733 until his death. In addition to his many secular activities, he served as a church musician in Rhode Island and South Carolina.

## Selby

William Selby (1738-98) was well known in London as an organist and composer when he came to America in 1771. He engaged in a wide variety of musical activities, including the promoting of a concert series in Boston that indirectly led to the founding of the Handel and Haydn Society in 1815.

## Reinagle

The most effective foreign-born (English) musician of this period was Alexander Reinagle (1756-1809). He was primarily a pianist and harpsichordist and was strongly interested in the theater. His only major semi-sacred composition was an uncompleted oratoric based upon Milton's *Paradise Lost*. Since his effect upon colonial culture was great, he undoubtedly made an indirect impression upon church music and musicians.

## Taylor

Raynor Taylor (1747-1825), another Englishman, was a teacher and an associate of Reinagle's. Despite his reputation as a convivial vaudeville performer, his musical ability carried

[2] See Leonard Ellinwood, *The History of American Church Music* (New York: Morehouse-Gorham Company, 1953), pp. 43 ff.

him into varied situations, including the position of organist in St. Peter's Church, Philadelphia. He was a master at improvisation and an exceedingly prolific composer, though his works are not presently in use. He is best remembered for having assisted in the founding of the Musical Fund Society of Philadelphia in 1820.

### Carr

Benjamin Carr (1768-1831) was also born in England, arriving in America in 1793. He was a singer but was best known as an organist and as co-founder of the Musical Fund Society. He composed numerous instrumental and vocal selections, including a collection of sacred music for use in Catholic churches.

### Van Hagen and Hewitt

Peter van Hagen (1750-1830) came from Rotterdam to Charleston, South Carolina, in 1774, later moving to New York and then to Boston with his musical family. James Hewitt (1770-1827) was born in England and came to New York in 1792. His family and the Van Hagens were popular musicians of their time but left little for succeeding generations except voluminous news clippings.

### first American composers

Francis Hopkinson is often said to have been the first American composer. He was deeply interested in church music, serving at various times as organist, director, and composer. His first handwritten collection, which he started in 1759, included a psalm setting and an anthem, both written in two parts. He wrote *A Letter to the Rev. Dr. White on the Conduct of a Church Organ*—a dissertation on the basic values of church music. One statement could have been written today: "It is as offensive to hear lilts and jigs from a church organ, as it would be to see a venerable matron frisking through

57

the public street with all the fantastic airs of a *Columbine*." [3]

Hopkinson composed a great deal of secular and sacred music but little of his work is alive today. He composed at least one oratorio and many songs. He published *A Collection of Psalm Tunes, with a few Anthems and Hymns* (1763). He also produced the *Psalms of David*, a collection of Genevan tunes, in 1767 and edited the hymn tunes for the Protestant Episcopal hymnal (1785).

James Lyon (1735-94), rather than Hopkinson, may have been the first American composer—or it could have been any one of several others, known or unknown. Lyon was a Presbyterian minister whose interest in music and the church led him to the publication of *Urania, or a choice collection of Psalm Tunes* in Philadelphia (1762). The book was quite popular; a second edition appeared in 1767, and a third in 1773. Six of the tunes were composed by Lyons; another, called "Whitfield," is commonly known today as the tune to "America."

## Flagg

Josiah Flagg (1738-ca. 94) was popular as a composer and promoter. His fame today rests primarily upon his book *A Collection of the best Psalm Tunes* printed by Paul Revere in 1764.

## Read

Daniel Read (1757-1836) was born in poverty and died in wealth. He composed a great deal and published a number of influential collections and books on music. He started *The American Musical Magazine*, a monthly publication.

## fuguing tunes

The fuguing tune which appeared during the last half of the century was a kind of counterpoint that resembled certain

[3] Chase, *op. cit.*, p. 101.

58

early forms of the sixteenth century. It is not a fugue such as

**Billings**

J. S. Bach might have written. The most famous exponent of the fuguing tune was William Billings (1746-1800), a Boston tanner turned musician, who had little or no training in his chosen field. He was possessed of boundless ability, considerable energy, and, like Isaac Watts, a misshapen body. He probably studied the most popular theory book of his day, Tans'ur's *Musical Grammar*, which was first published in England in 1734 with the title *The Complete Melody, or Harmony of Zion*. The American edition was published in 1767. His ideas about harmony and other aspects of musical theory seem to have been based upon those of Tans'ur.

Billings published a number of books and collections, some of which were quite popular and influential. His collections contained psalm and hymn tunes, anthems and canons, that were intended for use by choral societies and choirs. A number of his anthems have been re-issued in recent years. They have a crude but natural beauty that is quite appealing to many singers and listeners.

**shape notes**

Shape-note music, an interesting innovation of the late eighteenth century, was given its strongest and perhaps its initial boost by Andrew Law (1748-1821), a well-educated Connecticut minister. He had inserted in the 1781 edition of Watts' *Psalms of David, Imitated* sixteen pages of tunes which were printed with notes in the shape of a diamond, a square, a circle, or a triangle, each of which had a pitch designation very much like the previously mentioned fasola system. His shape-note tunes may have been previously published. He used every available means to promote his idea, which some authorities credit to William Little and William Smith who presented a similar plan in their book, *The Easy Instructor*, published at various times, possibly as early as 1798. According to Percy Scholes (*The Oxford Companion to Music*, London: Oxford University Press, 1956, p. 569), the system had been popular in England prior to 1767 and was therefore not original with Law, or any other American.

## folk hymnody

During the last half of the eighteenth century a type of folk hymnody, as opposed to psalmody, appeared in rural areas and inland towns. Hymns and tunes that resemble the camp-meeting and so-called gospel songs of later generations became popular among the Methodists and Baptists, most of whom had relatively little education, musical or otherwise, and whose tastes in music and literature were of a different caliber from those of the Episcopalians and Congregationalists. The appeal was almost entirely to the emotions, and for that reason the songs had little lasting effect. They did, however, serve a purpose, because they answered the needs of a particular group at a particular time.

## Holden

It is fitting that this chapter should close with a brief discussion of Oliver Holden (1765-1844). While his influence was felt in the nineteenth century, his most effective publications were prepared—if not printed—before 1800: *Union Harmony* (1793); *The Massachusetts Compiler* (1795), a study of psalmody made with Hans Gram and Samuel Holyoke (1762-1820); and *Plain Psalmody* (1800). His third book, *Charlestown Collection*, appeared in 1803. Holden's fame was made secure by the one eighteenth-century American hymn tune now generally in use—"Coronation," usually heard with the words "All hail the power of Jesus' name."

# VII

# The Nineteenth Century in Europe

The break between sacred and secular music that appeared after 1750 became increasingly pronounced during the nineteenth century. Most "name" composers were interested in the

**Mendelssohn and Bach**

concert hall and the theater. Their concern for sacred music was incidental, as is well illustrated by the "Bach Revival," whose chief sponsor was Felix Mendelssohn (1809-47). He was interested in Bach the musician. The fact that the passions, the great *B minor Mass*, the *Magnificat*, the organ works, and other compositions had been intended for use in the church was not particularly important to him or to his peers. Mendelssohn himself composed a little sacred music, the best being his "church pieces" for solos and chorus and his organ sonatas. His oratorios are in an entirely different category and will be discussed later.

**limitations imposed**

Nineteenth-century German composers are not to be criticized for the church music hiatus. Because of violent Lutheran opposition to anything that carried the slightest hint of the theatrical, an extreme attitude developed which surrounded church music with severe limitations. J. S. Bach had felt the pressure of these limitations, but he was strong enough to ignore them. He was, however, regularly in trouble with his superiors because of his refusal to bow to their demands. This rigid opposition to the strengthening of the church with music of depth and real beauty is only one of many such conflicts that have arisen from time to time. The holiness of beauty was again denied.

## disagreement among churches

Another factor that added to musical confusion was the lack of agreement among and within Protestant denominations in matters pertaining to worship—philosophy, structure, desired effects, and the like—and the resultant scattering of influence that drove many musicians away from the church. Only those composers who bowed to the popular demands of romanticism were given encouragement, but little of their music has endured. Sentimentality was the rule, solidarity the exception. Mendelssohn tried, unsuccessfully to re-introduce to the church the musical attitudes of Bach and his predecessors. He composed a number of motets and psalms using both orchestra and chorus. Musically he was successful—the psalms are especially well planned—but from the standpoint of influence he failed completely.

## Catholic music

Catholic music was less restrained and generally more effective, but its influence was not great. Major works such as Beethoven's Mass in D (Missa Solemnis) and Berlioz' two settings of the Te Deum were too "colossal" (Berlioz' word) for use in the church, being instead designed for concert performances. Luigi Cherubini (1760-1842) and Franz Schubert (1797-1828) contributed excellent settings of the mass, the former in Paris and the latter in Vienna.

Franz Liszt (1811-86) became quite excited about church music from time to time. Unfortunately his masses and psalms, though interesting and often thrilling, are not always churchly. In this, as in his private life, he was a frustrated man.

## Gounod and Franck

Two other French romanticists, Charles Gounod (1818-93) and César Franck (1822-90) wrote considerable sacred music. Their choral works are strongly tinged with secularism and are emotional to the point of being musically vulgar. Gounod's "O divine Redeemer" is one of the least objectionable of his songs. Gabriel-Urbain Fauré (1845-1924) is best known for his *Requiem*, which has considerable strength despite its romantic quality. *The Seven Last Words of Christ*, by Théodore Dubois (1837-1924), is extremely sentimental but still retains a large popular following among certain groups of people.

## Bruckner

Of all the nineteenth-century Catholic composers, the Austrian, Anton Bruckner (1824-96) rates highest. His psalms and masses are great music by any standard and have that spirituality which is the definitive quality of true church music.

## Rossini and Verdi

Gioacchino Rossini (1792-1868) and Giuseppe Verdi (1813-1901) are known to the general public for their operas. Each, however, composed sacred music which alone could have insured their fame. Their masses and shorter works are colorful and strongly romantic, but without the excessive sentimentality of most nineteenth-century sacred music.

## Grieg

The great Norwegian composer Edvard Grieg (1843-1907) wrote occasionally for the church. A number of famous Rus-

## Russian choral composers

sians composed liturgical music which has been translated and edited for use by Protestant choirs. Dimitri Bortniansky (1752-1825) was the earliest. His influence was stronger after he became director of the Imperial Choir at St. Petersburg in 1796.

Others were Alexander Borodin (ca. 1833-87); Mily Balakirev (1836-1910); Peter I. Tchaikovsky (1840-93); Michael Ippolitov-Ivanov (1859-1935); Sergei Rachmaninoff (1873-1943).

## Dvorak

Czechoslovakia is represented by Antonin Dvorák (1841-1904), who composed a group of sacred solos (*Biblical Songs*) which are in the repertoire of most successful singers.

## Mendelssohn's oratorios

Mendelssohn's oratorios *St. Paul* (1836) and *Elijah* (1846) are undoubtedly among the greatest sacred works of nineteenth-century Protestant composers. He had been strongly influenced by Bach's music and by the oratorios of Handel. His efforts to carry on in this area were crowned with success. Although romantic in concept and execution, these oratorios have a rare combination of beauty and dignified strength. Their sincerity and spiritual depth cannot be questioned.

## oratorios

The same cannot always be said for other nineteenth century composers of oratorio, including César Franck (*Beatitudes*), Charles Gounod (*Redemption*), and Hector Berlioz (*The Infant Christ*). The last named is an interesting composition and delightful to hear—in a concert hall. Ludwig Spohr (1784-1859) and Franz Liszt also produced oratorios, but not of any significance. These composers may have lacked Mendelssohn's understanding of good taste; it is certain that they lacked his ability.

## Brahms

Johannes Brahms (1833-97) limited his sacred choral compositions to shorter forms than did Mendelssohn and others. One of his greatest choral compositions is often called a secular anthem—*Song of Fate*, based on a poem by Friederich Hölderlein. His *German Requiem* is not liturgical in any sense, but it is truly sacred. The impact of either of these two works, when presented correctly and musically, cannot be described; it can only be felt. He wrote several other works of somewhat similar nature and numerous excellent short pieces. *Four Serious Songs* are equally effective in concert and in church if sung by a sensitive artist; his choral preludes are in every organist's repertoire. Brahms' sacred compositions are equal to those of any composer of any period and are excelled by none. It is unfortunate that he was given relatively little encouragement by the church.

## degenerate English music

The quality of nineteenth-century church music in England slipped to a new low. Of all the many anthem composers only a few deserve to be mentioned: John Goss (1800-1880), a competent organist whose music is ordinary at best; Thomas Walmisley (1814-56), also a fine organist—possibly because of his great interest in Bach; Arthur Sullivan (1842-1900), famous for his excellent secular music but unable to transfer that excellence to his service music; Joseph Barnby (1838-96), successful organist and director, who let sentimentality rule his composing; John Stainer (1840-1901), another successful organist and director, whose music at times was almost good (his *Crucifixion* is still quite popular despite its lush and sentimental romanticism); Samuel Sebastian Wesley (1810-76), son of Samuel Wesley and grandson of Charles Wesley, an excellent musician and a fine composer whose music shows his concern for Purcell, Byrd, and Tallis. Wesley is the only nineteenth-century English composer who deserves to be mentioned with the German masters.

## English hymn writers

English hymn writers of the romantic era produced poetry that ranged in quality from the ridiculous to the sublime. The sublime was obvious in the works of Reginald Heber (1783-1826), whose poetry was equal in the minds of many to that of Byron and Shelley. Eighteenth-century hymnody had been dominated by the desire of Watts, Wesley, and their less effective imitators to produce hymns that the uneducated masses could understand and enjoy. It was inevitable that a demand would arise from more cultured levels for something to supplement and partially replace the metrical psalms. Bishop Heber was one of several who answered the demand. His "The Son of God goes forth to war," "Bread of the world" and "Holy, holy, holy!" are representative of the many fine hymns he wrote during a short but highly productive lifetime.

Among others who made similar contributions were Thomas Kelly (1769-1854, "Look, ye saints!"); James Montgomery, a Scottish Moravian (1771-1854, "Hail to the Lord's Annointed" and "O Spirit of the Living God"); John Keble, who will be discussed in connection with the Oxford Movement (1792-1866, "Sun of my soul, Thou Saviour dear"); Henry Francis Lyte, whose most popular hymns provide an excellent summary of his life (1793-1847, "Jesus, I my cross have taken," "Praise, my soul, the King of Heaven," and "Abide with me"); John Bowring (1792-1872, "In the cross of Christ I glory" and "God is love. His mercy brightens"); Charlotte Elliott, less scholarly than some of the others and a bit more emotional (1789-1871, "Just as I am," "My God, my Father, while I stray").

## English hymn tunes

Hymn-tune composers of the early nineteenth century failed to match the standards demanded by the better texts. Generally speaking, the tunes were of three types—psalm tunes, "Methodist tunes," and instrumental borrowings. The first named needs no further discussion. "Methodist tunes" was a catchall name given to the popular melodies used by Methodists, Baptists, and others to carry their evangelistic poetry. A few of these had enough solid value to live, but most did not. However, the general quality was considerably above that of similar tunes of the preceding century. For example, "Diadem" (ca. 1840) is not a bad tune despite its deficiencies. Dozens of tune books were published between 1800 and 1850. Many contained good tunes as well as others of less value. A real effort was being made to interest congregations in a more effective, satisfying kind of hymn singing. The movement was aided by the establishment of singing schools and by the increasing attention being given to choirs.

The third type—instrumental borrowings—produced some laughable misfits. The tendency to believe that music by Mendelssohn, Haydn, or Beethoven will automatically make good hymn tunes is not unknown even today. Almost none of the instrumental misfits lasted long as hymn tunes.

## Oxford Movement

The Oxford Movement was the most significant factor affecting nineteenth-century English church music—the entire church for that matter. It was the result of efforts made by leaders and laymen, partially as a reaction to the evangelical revival, to bring the Anglican Church out of an era of lethargy, despondency, and degradation. John Keble preached a sermon at Oxford on July 14, 1833 that was a calculated attempt to arouse the church to its condition. Others accepted the challenge and the movement was under way. It was basically an

## Tractarians

attempt to "purify" the church by returning to the "divine origin" concept. In an effort to popularize their ideas, the promoters circulated pamphlets or "tracts" in considerable quantity, thereby giving themselves the sometimes derogatory name of "Tractarians." The direction taken by its leaders caused many of them to go beyond Keble's philosophy to the extent that they joined the Roman Catholic Church. Those who remained Anglican accomplished some of the original aims of rejuvenation.

One of the characteristics of the Oxford Movement was the return to a philosophy of worship that made it possible for beauty to assume its rightful place in the church. The rituals were re-examined with a view toward re-creating the age-old patterns that had served so well at various times and in various places. An orderly, liturgical service became the goal.

A byproduct of this concern for order and beauty was the

**boy choirs**

attention given to choirs and congregations. The increased use of boy choirs—and the establishment of choir schools—the use of vestments and processionals, and sung services gave choirs a position of importance. Congregational music profited from the efforts of hymn writers who turned to the church, the Sacraments, and the Christian year for subject matter, and translators who brought into English verse the ancient prayers and poetry of the historical Christian faith.

John Mason Neale (1818-66) was one of the most influential contributors to the movement, primarily because of his interest in Greek and Roman hymns which he translated into excellent English poetry. "O come, O come, Immanuel," "Good Christian men, rejoice," "Christian! dost thou see them" and "Come, ye faithful, raise the strain" are representative. His work aroused others who added more usable translations. In addition, Neale wrote a number of fine hymns, including "Art thou weary," which he at first called a translation.

Unlike Neale, who remained Anglican, some Oxford hymn

68

writers became Roman Catholics. Of these, John Henry Newman (1801-90, "Lead, kindly Light"); Edward Caswell, who is best known for his translations of Latin hymns (1814-78, "When morning gilds the skies"); and Frederick W. Faber (1814-63, "Faith of our fathers!") were perhaps the most influential.

Neale was not alone in his loyalty to the Anglican Church. There were many influential writers who came to be known as Anglican Catholics. Mrs. Cecil Alexander (1818-95) was greatly interested in the religious growth of children. However, most of her hymns, such as "There is a green hill far away," are hardly appropriate for children. Her "All things bright and beautiful" is one of the few in current use.

Several other high-churchmen deserve to be mentioned. Among them are Christopher Wordsworth (1807-85, "O Lord of heaven and earth and sea"); Henry Baker (1821-77, "The King of Love my Shepherd is"); Folliott Pierpoint (1835-1917, "For the beauty of the earth"); Edward Plumptre (1821-91, "Rejoice, ye pure in heart"); and Samuel Stone (1839-1900, "The Church's one foundation").

Composers of hymn tunes did not respond immediately to

**hymn-tune collection**

the Oxford Movement. W. H. Havergal (1793-1870) published a new edition of the old Ravenscroft psalm tunes (1844). His preface gave some indication of new trends, which were even more pronounced in his own Old Church Psalmody (1847). He avoided all tunes of pietistic sentimentality as well as those classified as "Methodist tunes." These books, and others of similar nature, are not significant for their musical quality but for the somewhat abrupt shift which they made toward a more solid kind of hymn tune. Relatively few of the new tunes remained alive for long.

## Hymns Ancient and Modern

The great music publishing event of the century was the appearance in 1861 of the tune book for *Hymns Ancient and Modern*. Texts only were published in 1859 as a small trial book, then enlarged in 1860, again in 1868, and finally presented as a complete hymnal in 1875. Other editions have followed, the last in 1950. Generations of church musicians, ministers, and congregations have made *H A and M* the most influential hymnbook ever published. The editors had succeeded in producing a rare collection, a combination of practicality and reasonably high standards.

It is not to be assumed that the tunes written for *H A and M* (1861) were all perfect or that all were even good tunes.

## Dykes

Actually, only a few lived past 1900. The most popular were those of John B. Dykes (1823-76). His earliest works were generally quite good. "Nicaea" ("Holy, holy, holy!"), one of his best, was written in 1860 or 1861. His later efforts are inclined to be shallow, overly harmonized, and very emotional. The 1875 *H A and M* included seventy-five Dykes tunes. He fell victim to his own success.

## Sullivan and Barnby

Two other "names" of the times, Arthur Sullivan and Joseph Barnby, followed the same inviting road to eventual musical destruction. Sullivan is saved from oblivion by his secular works—Gilbert and Sullivan operettas—but his hymn tunes were so much in accord with the sentimentality of his day that they are virtually forgotten. Barnby composed about three hundred tunes. A few are strongly alive, possibly because of association with good texts—"O perfect love" and "Laudes Domini" ("When morning gilds the skies").

H. J. Gauntlett (1805-76) should be mentioned because he

is said to have composed ten thousand hymn tunes. ". . . certainly his material is in the main beaten out thin enough to make that possible. He neither blusters like Wesley [S. S.], sobs like Sullivan or croons like Dykes. At his best he is a true and inspired master of the commonplace. . . ." [1]

## Samuel S. Wesley

The best tunes of the Victorian age were written by the best church musician, Samuel S. Wesley. He composed and arranged perhaps two hundred tunes, most of them of a caliber considerably above those of his contemporaries. He avoided the pitfalls of excessive popularity and gained lasting respect instead. "Aurelia," frequently associated with "The Church's one foundation," is one of his most effective tunes.

It is unfortunate that the great mass of hymn tunes other than those in *H A and M* were generally less than mediocre. The musical situation was further disturbed because there had been a great revival of interest in congregational singing and every denomination had set out to help the revival with its own collection. Sources of tunes were many and varied, but only those melodies that had already stood the test of time can be classed with the best of those found in *H A and M*.

The evangelical movement within and without the Anglican Church was not related to the Oxford Movement, yet was influenced by it. Hymn writers attempted to maintain reasonably high standards, and the tunes, while far from great, were generally acceptable. Texts were quite personal, as in Arabella Katherine Hankey's (1834-1911) "I love to tell the story," and in George Croly's (1780-1860) "Spirit of God, descend upon my heart." One of the most prolific writers of this group was Frances Havergal (1836-79), who might be called an Anglican

---

[1] Routley, *The Music of Christian Hymnody*, p. 126.

71

evangelist. "Take my life" and "Lord, speak to me" are two representative examples of her better hymns.

Midway between the high church and the evangelical attitudes was a group of writers who were "scientific low-churchmen." They liked Anglican-Catholic philosophy, but recognized the need for its modernization in terms of contemporary social philosophies. The leaders in this area were intellectual hymnists, and the hymns they wrote reflect their dual person-

### How, Ellerton, and Tennyson

alities. William How (1823-97), known as the "poor man's bishop," wrote for the uneducated, but he did not write down to them. "For all the saints," "O Word of God Incarnate," and "O Jesus, Thou art standing" are good hymns that have increased in popularity with every generation. John Ellerton (1826-93, "Saviour, again to thy dear name we raise,") was equally prolific and was successful in combining good texts with easy-to-understand concepts. Alfred Tennyson (1809-92) wrote no hymns as such, but several, such as "Strong Son of God, immortal love," have been lifted out of his long poems.

### Scottish hymnody

The Presbyterian Church in Scotland held fast to the restrictions imposed by Calvinistic doctrine until the middle of the nineteenth century. No hymns appeared until 1839; organs were forbidden prior to 1874; and no hymnal was published until 1898. The gradual loosening of restrictions came as a result of an evangelistic movement and the establishment of several dissenting churches. All factions were reunited and became The Church of Scotland in 1929.

### Bonar

Horatius Bonar (1808-89) is often called the greatest Scottish writer of hymns. His works reflect an evangelistic fervor, as in "Go, labor on!" and "I heard the voice of Jesus say." The latter was written for children. Of the many other Scottish hymn writers, two deserve at least to be mentioned: Elizabeth Clephane (1830-69, "Rock of ages"); and George Matheson (1842-1906, "O Love that wilt not let me go").

Various English dissenting groups contributed hymns which are still alive; Sarah Flower Adams (1805-48) wrote "Nearer, my God, to Thee." She, like John Wreford (1800-81, "Lord, while for all mankind we pray"), was a Unitarian.

## Julian's dictionary

The second great publishing event of the century was the appearance in London in 1892 of *A Dictionary of Hymnology*. Editor John A. Julian (1839-1913) assembled a staff of writers who contributed more than 1,500 items to the book, which has come to be known as *Julian's Dictionary*. The second edition in 1907 included a supplement. Dover Publications of New York brought out a two-volume edition (not a revision) in 1957.

## organs

The ups and downs of hymns and tunes were equaled by variations in the quality of organs, organist, and organ music. A few composers maintained reasonably high, even excellent,

## Franck

standards. César Franck belongs in this group, for, unlike his choral music, his organ compositions are considered by many to be good music; much of it usable in the church. His status as a composer is not firmly established, but it seems reasonably safe to say that he devoted more of his time to the church than any famous musician since Bach.

## Guilmant and Widor

Franck's contemporaries Alexandre Guilmant (1837-1911)

and Charles-Marie Widor (1845-1937) composed organ music that is used extensively today.

Much nineteenth-century organ music is inferior to that of

**"orchestral" organs**

the eighteenth and twentieth centuries. The organ became a victim of its own excellence. Mechanical improvements, particularly the invention of pneumatic and, later, electric action, made possible the development of the so-called "orchestral" organ which attempted to place the tone color of an orchestra in the hands of one person. Because polyphonic music did not lend itself to the effective expression of many romantic concepts, it was shoved aside in favor of harmonic structures. It is only in recent years that organ builders and organists have regained a more sensible attitude toward this great instrument.

Nineteenth-century church music in Europe was undergoing a period of excitement and dullness, of searching and stagnation. Fortunately the emphasis during the last two or three decades was upon excitement and searching. The greatest need was—and still is—to discover what the excitement was all about and for what the search was being made.

# VIII

# The Century of Mason and Moody

## Mason

Lowell Mason (1792-1872) was the most influential of all nineteenth-century American musicians. His work in churches and public schools affected not only his generation, but all generations to come. Mason was a successful businessman who resisted the appeal of his avocation—music—as long as possible. When he capitulated he went all the way and gave himself completely to composing, teaching, editing, and promoting. It is unfortunate that of the four he was least capable as editor and composer.

Mason came from a musical family in a musical community, Medfield, Massachusetts. His grandfather had been a singing-school teacher. Mason probably received his first training—outside his family—in a singing school. He became a competent organist and was able to play several other instruments. He moved to Savannah in 1812 where he combined business (banking) with pleasure (church organist). His earliest compositions and arrangements were published as the *Boston Handel and Haydn Society Collection of Church Music* in 1821(?), without giving him credit. Mason did not care for his business associates to know of his venturing so far afield. In 1827 he accepted a position as choirmaster in a Boston church, and another as a teller in a bank.

Mason's interest in music for children dates from his early

Savannah days. He published his *Juvenile Psalmist* in 1829 and *The Child's Introduction to Sacred Music* in 1830. He obtained the help of others to found and operate the Boston Academy of Music (1832-47), where free music instruction was given to thousands of children and adults. He believed strongly that music was for everyone.

Mason composed and arranged a great deal of music, espe-

**European influence**

cially hymn tunes. While his publications contained works of Americans, he leaned strongly toward European composers. He attempted to eliminate "popular" American music, including "fuguing pieces." Unfortunately, his use of tunes selected from the works of "name" composers did not necessarily make more good sacred music available to the public. It has previously been emphasized that music chosen from a Beethoven, Haydn, or Mozart concerto, quartet, or symphony may make very poor hymn or anthem tunes.

Mason's concern seemed often to have been for superficial appearance rather than musical and textual sincerity and solidarity. The techniques of public performance, of singing, and of playing were quite important to him. It is not too much to say that he applied many of the techniques of Phineas Barnum to church and school music. His concept of music in worship put a severe strain on efforts to maintain the holiness of beauty.

Despite his interest in showmanship, Mason made a valuable contribution to American musical life. He opened the eyes of his generation to the value of music for everyone in church and school. He composed many hymn tunes that were easy to sing. Although the tunes are in the sentimental mood of his times, they helped carry church music through a time of active encroachment by factors that were far from elevating, either spiritually or musically. Many Mason tunes are still in common use. The number, however, is decreasing with each generation. Had he shown less interest in European musicians and given more encouragement to American composers, he would undoubtedly be held in much higher esteem today. His inclination to consider anything European to be of superior quality may have been due to two factors: (1) His first real music teacher was a German, F. L. Abel, whom he met in Savannah about 1812; (2) for various political and economic reasons a veritable flood of European performers and teachers, many of very high caliber, came to America during the first half of the century. Their influence on the cultural life of this brawling, sprawling country cannot be overlooked.

Mason's contemporaries turned out enormous quantities of music that, at its best, was mediocre. Thomas Hastings (1784-1872, "Toplady") composed perhaps a thousand tunes and published fifty volumes of music. Four or five of his tunes are alive today. George Webb (1803-87, "Webb"); William Bradbury (1816-68, "Olive's Brow"); Henry K. Oliver (1800-1885, "Federal Street"); Isaac Woodbury (1819-58, "Selena"); and George F. Root (1820-95, "Varina") were some of the other more prolific composers.

Recent studies of the singing-school movement that spread through the South between 1800 and 1850 have uncovered the real American music of this period. It is unfortunate that Mason and his educated peers so casually dismissed the works of Billings and others who developed the "fuguing tune." The possibilities of working with the advocates of American music were completely overlooked by the very persons who might have done something with it. (In England Boyce was guilty of the same offense in the seventeenth century when he ignored Tallis, Tye, and Purcell.)

Church music was not alone in being dominated by European composers. The New York Philharmonic Society guaranteed the performance of one American work every season, provided an examining committee gave its approval. Non-European composers labored long and fruitlessly to obtain an adequate hearing for their compositions.

## fasola and shape notes

Southern musicians developed a separate kind of music based on the fasola system previously mentioned. Shape notes were accepted as the standard—four notes, as advocated by Andrew Law and others, and another system which gave one note for each of the seven steps of the diatonic scale. The style of singing resembled the highly ornamented psalm singing of early New England days. Incidentally, this same style is still popular in certain areas, especially those that continue to use *The Sacred Harp*, a collection first published in 1844. (Collections using either four or seven shaped-note patterns are being published today.)

The most successful advocate of the four-note system of shape notes was John Wyeth (1770-1858), whose collection *Repository of Sacred Music* (1810) was widely used. Later publications of a similar nature were strongly influenced by Wyeth's book. (See Chase, *America's Music*, pp. 186 ff., for a detailed discussion of "The Fasola Folk.") Shape-note hymns were folklike in character, often resembling popular folk songs of the day. George Pullen Jackson (1874-1953) and others have done much research in this relatively unknown area of American music. The inter-relationship of sacred and secular tunes and white and Negro spirituals is being given serious consideration by musicologists. Much remains to be discovered. (See Jackson, *White Spirituals of the Southern*

*Uplands* [Chapel Hill: The University of North Carolina Press, 1933].)

**camp-meeting song**

Parallel to, and to a certain extent, interdependent with fasola music was the camp-meeting song. The first camp meeting is said to have been held in 1800 in Logan County, Kentucky. The participants in this and later similar affairs had no knowledge of music; many had no education at all. It was necessary that their songs be musically and textually simple. The system of "lining-out" was used extensively, and the singing was enthusiastic if not technically good. Thousands of songs and dozens of song collections were written and published to serve the needs of the people. Only a few lasted for long, but the philosophy of the camp-meeting (gospel) song carried over into later periods and was given worldwide impetus in the Moody-Sankey evangelistic movement.

Early camp-meeting songs, like those of the fasola singers, were folklike and, strange to say, possessed characteristics not unlike those of the works of William Billings and his associates. The music that "educated" leaders had abandoned showed its inherent strength by continuing to live among the uncultured, "natural" musicians of the South.

One interesting characteristic of camp-meeting singing was that the tune was almost always sung by high male voices. Female voices sang in harmony above the melody, and because no one had told them they could not sing high, in their uninhibited fashion they sang notes far above the accepted limits set by a twentieth-century congregation. Singing was enjoyed, but only incidentally because it was used primarily as a means of conversion and as an outlet for repressions. (See Chase, *America's Music*, Chapter 11, and especially p. 223.)

The influence of gospel songs was great and widespread. Mason and his contemporaries included a few in their collections. Because gospel song books contained words and music, often printed together, the various denominations were forced to publish "official" hymn-and-tune books, much against the wishes of their leaders who preferred to have all texts in one book and tunes in another. It was their contention, and rightly so, that a hymn was a poem. Their mistake was in underestimating the power of a tune to strengthen or weaken the text. After 1850 the trend moved strongly toward the equally false view that the tune was more important than the text. One factor that distinguished, and continues to distinguish, gospel songs from hymns is the relative importance of tune and text. In the former the tune is almost always strongly dominant. In the latter the text is slightly dominant, but the tune is accepted as a vitally important part of what is often termed a musical marriage.

Sacred songs of the people have always existed in one form or another. The nineteenth-century gospel song was recognized by evangelistic groups as a powerful device to use in increasing the effectiveness of the evangelistic service—the direct de-

**Sankey**

scendant of the camp meeting. The most famous exponent of the gospel song, Ira D. Sankey (1840-1908), combined his singing and tune-writing abilities (1871-99) with the preaching of Dwight L. Moody to make America and Europe gospel-song conscious. Sankey's tunes were sentimental and very simple; their appeal came from a folklike unpretentiousness that is even today a pleasant relief from the mediocrity of Mason and his peers. Very few Sankey tunes lasted for long, possibly because floods of new gospel songs have been produced for each generation, and always in the musical and textual idiom popular at the time. "I am praying for you" and "The ninety and nine" are in a few denominational hymnals.

The "special" music of the nineteenth century was affected with increasing intensity by the gradual encroachment of the mixed quartet, which sometimes was the only choral group in the church, or sometimes part of a choir (the quartet-choir). Anthems were expected to contain solos, duets, quartets, and a small bit for the entire choir. The most successful composer in this medium was Dudley Buck (1839-1909) who turned out great quantities of pseudo-Wagnerian compositions. He and his associates were partially responsible for the separation that occurred between 1850 and 1910 of church music from worship. The emphasis was upon vocal and instrumental showmanship more or less in the style of opera and the concert stage. Buck wrote a number of extended works, including sacred and secular cantatas and several settings of the *Te Deum*. His compositions have retained their popularity until recent times and are heard occasionally today.

## influence of Oxford Movement

Indirectly the Oxford Movement in England was responsible for the eventual return of a more effective union of music and worship in America. The revival of interest in England in planned services that depended heavily upon the leadership of a well-trained choir proved to be contagious. The American Protestant Episcopal Church turned to the almost forgotten male choir, establishing numerous choir schools as far west as Chicago. Vestments were introduced, over considerable opposition, and processionals were again accepted as part of the service. The contrast between a service that permitted orderliness and beauty to contribute to worship and the theatrical effusions found in many churches was so obvious that other denominations slowly but surely made adjustments which eventually led to the restoration of music to its rightful place in the church. The boy-choir movement attained its peak between 1890 and 1910, but its place has been more than adequately filled by other singing groups.

## Paine

John K. Paine (1839-1906) was the first American composer to attain stature among Europeans. He was an excellent organist, a competent composer, and an effective teacher of music at Harvard from 1862-1906. While his music is no longer used, his students have carried on the tradition of high artistic standards that he followed, and their influence has been considerable. He overcame a great deal of academic opposition to gain a firm place for music in the American college curriculum.

American hymn writers of the nineteenth century were more successful than their musical opposites in producing

## Dwight

works of lasting value. Timothy Dwight has been previously mentioned as the first American to write a long-lived hymn. Many of the hymnals published between 1800 and 1850 were

## hymn collections

primarily extensions of and additions to Watts' *Psalms and Hymns*. Each editor managed to insert a few new hymns, often his own. The hymns of eighteenth-century English poets were increasingly evident, especially selections from the *Olney Hymns* of Cowper and Newton. The earliest attempt made by the Protestant Episcopal Church at publishing a hymnal (1790) was not entirely successful. Boston's Trinity Church succeeded with its own hymnal of 1808. The first complete Protestant Episcopal hymnal approved by the denomination was published in 1827. George W. Doane (1799-1859) contributed two hymns to the collection. He has three in common use today, "Softly now the light of day" being perhaps the most popular.

Other denominations published official hymnals, and literally hundreds appeared that had no official backing. Most gospel songbooks were in the latter category. Editors often included in the title a statement which could imply approval: "Prepared for the use of the _____ Church."

### Unitarian hymn writers

The Unitarians in America were actively opposed to anything Calvinistic. Their hymns were generally excellent, and many are still very much alive. Two writers of hymns and poetry merit special mention: Oliver W. Holmes (1809-94, "Lord of all being") and Samuel Longfellow (1819-92, "Holy spirit, Truth divine"). James R. Lowell (1819-91) was not a member of the church, but his writings are not antagonistic toward Unitarian beliefs. His "Once to every man and nation" consists of lines selected from *The Present Crisis*.

### Whittier

Another great American poet, John Greenleaf Whittier (1807-92), wrote no hymns, but some of his poetry has been converted to hymns. "O brother man," "I know not what the future hath," "Dear Lord and Father of mankind," and others are portions of poems which are less well known than the hymns derived from them.

There are many whose hymns attained lasting success, and many more for whom fame was fleeting. Only the more significant writers can be mentioned here: Ray Palmer (1808-87, "My faith looks up to Thee"); Mary A. Lathbury (1841-1913, "Break thou the bread of life"); Elizabeth Prentiss (1818-78, "More love to Thee, O Christ"); Edward Hopper (1816-88, "Jesus, Saviour, pilot me"); Phillips Brooks (1835-93, "O little town of Bethlehem"); Maltbie Babcock (1858-

1901, "This is my Father's world"); Washington Gladden (1836-1918, "O Master, let me walk with Thee"); and Fannie Crosby (1820-1915, "Rescue the perishing").

Nineteenth-century American church music wandered away in so many directions that real progress could not logically be expected. All the promise at the end of the eighteenth century of great things to come was smothered by an overwhelming surge of mediocrity from which church music is only now beginning to recover.

# IX

# The Twentieth Century in Europe

The music of today has its roots deeply embedded in the past. "Modern" music has existed in every age, but never has it been completely separated from the works of preceding generations. Twentieth-century music seems to have broken rather abruptly with the immediate past—the Romantic period—but actually the changes have occurred in a logical sequence. Just as Beethoven made the transition from Haydn and Mozart to Schumann and Brahms, so Richard Strauss (1864-1949) in Germany, and Claude Debussy (1862-1918) in France, provided leadership in examining the inadequacies of previous concepts.

It is unfortunate that of all the great musicians of the transitional period from 1890 to 1910 only two gave much of their

**Vaughan Williams and Holst**

time and interest to church music. The Englishmen Ralph Vaughan Williams (1872-1958) and Gustav Holst (1874-1934) could stand in the company of the greatest, and their influence upon church music would be difficult to overemphasize. Edward Elgar (1857-1934), also English, wrote some church music, but like Arthur Sullivan, was unable to transfer his skill and artistry in secular music to his sacred compositions. Continental musicians, with the exception of organists, generally ignored church music. Their contributions were negligible.

Leadership in matters related to music, education, literature, and social development, as has been previously mentioned, passed into secular control during the eighteenth century. During the nineteenth century the church was content to dawdle along far in the rear. The camp-meeting song which said, "It was good for Paul and Silas and it's good enough for me" gives a fair measure of the attitude of most church-men—leaders and followers—toward music. The inertia developed by this attitude required considerable time and the unceasing efforts of a few dedicated musicians and ministers to overcome.

As is often the case, the man who had the courage of his convictions and who made the very rough but necessary attempt to loosen the stranglehold of Victorian English medi-ocrity—Robert Bridges (1844-1930)—found his own efforts **beginning of improvement**
to be less than entirely successful. His *Yattendon Hymnal* (1899), however, was so scholarly in structure, so beautiful in format, and so musically sound that the way was cleared for his successors to attain the goals he had established. Bridges was an outspoken, caustic critic of current practices in church music. His music editor, Harry Wooldridge (1845-1917), de-pended primarily upon old, solid melodies of past centuries—the works of Croft, Gibbons, Tallis, and others. Wooldridge's own tunes were of the same calibre. Bridges wrote many new hymns for old tunes and translated others from German, Greek, and Roman sources. That he was an excellent poet there is no doubt—he became England's Poet Laureate. Bridges' efforts were aided by those of the equally outspoken G. R. Woodward (1848-1934) whose *Songs of Syon* (1904) was a beautiful but uncompromising collection of old melodies —plainsong, psalm tunes, and Lutheran chorales—as nearly as possible in their original versions. The book was not a financial

86

success, but it did help to jar some people out of their complacency.

### revised H A and M

Complacency made one last fling, however, in the appearance in 1904 of a revised *Hymns Ancient and Modern*. The revision was complete; tunes were restored to their original structure; many poor tunes were eliminated; hymns were re-translated or re-edited. Despite all the changes in its makeup, the new *H A and M* attempted to hold too firmly to the past, and the changes only served to antagonize its old friends without making new ones.

A *Historical Edition of H A and M* was first published in 1909. There are 111 pages of rather small type devoted to a careful study of hymnology in general, twenty-seven pages about the hymn writers in *H A and M*, and twelve pages about the tune composers.

### Parry and Stanford

Charles Hubert Parry (1848-1918) and Charles Stanford (1852-1924) played dominant roles in the 1904 revision. Each was a successful musician. Parry composed several anthems that were romantic without being Victorian. He did not grind out great quantities of anthems or hymn tunes; each work was well written, logical, and scholarly, albeit a bit dry and uninteresting at times. Stanford, in contrast, composed boldly, combining the theatrical with his concept of solid church music. His tunes were sometimes like anthems and his anthems almost like opera—too colorful, too bold, too daring, perhaps, but never boring.

Vaughan Williams was able to do what many other famous composers had failed to do either because of disinterest or disability: He moved freely between secular and sacred music without loss of efficiency or prestige. He composed so widely

87

that it is possible to find one or more of his excellent works to suit almost any church situation. When he combined his talents with those of scholarly Percy Dearmer (1867-1936) to produce a new hymnal it was a foregone conclusion that the results would be spectacular, but in a solid, secure fashion.

## The English Hymnal

The *English Hymnal* (1906) seems to have finally brought the the Oxford Movement down to the level of the people by employing the relatively simple device of using many fine old folk tunes to which sacred words were given. Tunes were derived from other sources, it is true. Vaughan Williams' "Sine Nomine" is a good example of a tune composed for the collection. But the unique strength and great popular appeal of the hymnal was derived from its folk songs. Under the guidance of less competent persons the book could have been of such low calibre that its value would have been severely limited.

## competition

*Hymns Ancient and Modern* and the *English Hymnal* each attracted its own strong-voiced following. In an effort to regain slipping prestige the advocates of *H A and M* abandoned the 1904 edition in favor of a new and excellent supplement (1916) to the old *H A and M*, but the *English Hymnal* reigned supreme despite its inclusion of many hymns and tunes that were either of poor quality or in bad taste or both. Folk songs were not an unalloyed blessing, and not every hymnal has followed the lead in this direction.

## Songs of Praise

A significant outgrowth of the controversy between advocates of *H A and M* and *E H* was the publication of another collection, *Songs of Praise* (1926 and 1932). Martin (1875-1958) and Geoffrey (1879-1943) Shaw were influential in the preparation of this excellent hymnal. These famous brothers were primarily interested in teaching, and the book is very frankly intended to be a student hymnal. Its music and poetry are of such high calibre, however, that many congregations adopted it for regular use. The feature that appeals most to congregations is the dependence upon a natural kind of speech rhythm which, in turn, determines the structure of the tunes. The revised *English Hymnal* (1933) borrowed ninety-six tunes from *Songs of Praise*, added twenty-two from other sources, and left its hymn content unchanged.

Other denominations were inevitably affected by the improvements in Anglican hymnody. The *Methodist Hymnal* of 1932 contains a great deal of valuable material as well as many less effective items retained from previous collections.

## Parry and Routley

Kenneth L. Parry (1884-1962) was chairman of the committee which prepared *Congregational Praise* (1951). He and Erik Routley (1917-) compiled the *Companion to Congregational Praise* (1953), an excellent handbook for an excellent hymnal and a reliable source of information about hymns and tunes. *H A and M* was revised again in 1950, but its influence appears to be somewhat limited.

An interesting byproduct of the improvements in English church music has been the general acceptance of the church musician as a member of the "family." He is no longer looked upon as a necessary nuisance to be carefully controlled lest he produce something not entirely legal. He has become a valuable individual, encouraged to make his peculiar contribution to the enrichment of worship.

## Welsh music

The people of Wales are known for their love of singing. It is only in recent times, however, that their hymn tunes have been accepted by churchmen in other countries. There is a rhythmic and melodic unity about Welsh tunes that makes them delightful for congregational singing. Charles Hubert Parry and Ralph Vaughan Williams were of Welsh ancestry, but their tunes are not particularly nationalistic. Most typical Welsh tunes were either folk songs or the products of relatively little-known composers.

European hymn writers of the twentieth century have not made their influence felt as in the past. Future generations may discover great hymns written between 1900 and 1962

**Oxenham**

that are unknown or not accepted today. John Oxenham (ca. 1852-1941), who was born William A. Dunkerley, made a strong impression upon the church and the general public with his many publications. Servicemen during World War I sang from his *Hymns for Men at the Front*. His one hymn in current use is "In Christ there is no East or West," written in 1908.

**Bax**

Clifford Bax (1886-) is a successful writer in many areas, his greatest success being with musical plays. His "Turn back, O man, forswear thy foolish ways" is found in many hymnals.

**Dearmer**

Percy Dearmer is often called England's greatest hymnologist of the twentieth century. He was much more than a hymn writer and translator; he was a student of hymns. His association with Martin Shaw, organist of the church he served, was beneficial to both. Dearmer's influence was worldwide because of his extensive writings. He served as editor of several excellent collections, including the *Oxford Book of Carols*. Perhaps his most momentous accomplishment was the leadership he gave in helping to plan, edit, and promote the *English Hymnal* and, later, *Songs of Praise*. His handbook, *Songs of Praise Discussed* (1933), is an excellent and scholarly source of information.

A number of English writers and composers have made valuable contributions to church music but not necessarily as writers of hymns or composers of tunes. Among these per-

## Routley

sons Erik Routley stands out with increasing brilliance as he continues to publish critical works of inestimable value. He is a fortunate and rare combination of musician and scholar and is therefore able to write with confidence and authority. The titles of his books are a fair indication of the wide range of his interests: *The Wisdom of the Father, I'll Praise My Maker, Organist and Congregation, The Music of Christian Hymnody, The Church and Music, Hymns and Faith, Hymns and Human Life, The Gift of Conversion, The English Carol, Ecumenical Psalmody, Church Music and Theology, Ascent to the Cross, Music: Sacred and Profane.*

## Holst

Gustav Holst was a personal friend of Vaughan Williams and shared with him the responsibility of leading English music out of the doldrums of mediocrity in which it had lain so long. Holst has a few hymn tunes in current use; more may be accepted in future years. He is best known among church musicians for his excellent choral compositions, many being of a festival type. His compositions for chorus with instruments, even a full orchestra, are effective without being flamboyant.

## Walton and Britten

William Walton (1902-) and Benjamin Britten (1913-) are well established as composers of fine sacred choral music, the latter in both large and small forms.

A whole generation of excellent composers and performers of sacred music grew up under the influence of Vaughan

*other English composers*

Williams and Holst. Among them are Edward Bairstow (1874-1946), Gordon Jacob (1895-), Percy Whitlock (1903-46), John Ireland (1879-), Charles Wood (1866-1926).

*Milhaud, Honegger, Messiaen, and Alain*

A few twentieth-century French musicians composed significant sacred music on occasion: Darius Milhaud (1892-); Arthur Honegger (1892-1955), whose oratorio "King David" is increasingly popular. Olivier Messiaen (1908-) is best known for his organ compositions, as was Jehan Alain (1911-40).

*Stravinsky*

Among the many recent Slavic composers, only Igor Stravinsky (1882-) has shown serious interest in sacred music. His *Symphony of Psalms* is an important work. He has several smaller sacred compositions and a mass for chorus and orchestra. His ballet based on the story of Noah was first seen on television in 1962. Stravinsky became an American citizen shortly after World War II.

*Schonberg*

Arnold Schonberg (1874-1951) was born in Austria. In 1940 he too became an American citizen after establishing an international reputation. He composed several small sacred works and a biblical opera, *Moses and Aaron*. He failed to complete an oratorio, *Jacob's Ladder*.

The quality of church music in England and continental Europe seems to have improved since 1900 despite two terrible wars and the constant fear of a third. Better communication among all persons who are concerned with the use of music in the church will make continued improvement a certainty.

# The Twentieth Century in America

*viewpoints*

Writers are inclined to be either extremely optimistic or extremely pessimistic in their evaluation of American church music since 1900. I believe that neither view is correct. A fair evaluation of the total picture cannot be made because the distance in time is much too short. It is easy to concentrate on a small area and justify any extreme viewpoint.

*confusion*

The situation at the beginning of the century was one of confusion. Many large congregations listened each Sunday to the operatic effusions of a well-paid quartet whose concern for worship was often negligible. Others listened to equally operatic, but less efficient quartet choirs. Smaller congregations did their best to fall into line, using whatever talents were at hand. Choirs, where they existed, were often used for the display of talent, temperment, and jealousies— all to the detriment of the church. Music was not considered in terms of its relation to worship. Gospel songs, many of a very transient nature, were extremely popular. Official hymnals of certain denominations were having a rough time. Most of the holiness had fled from beauty, and beauty, in turn had disowned holiness. The one bright spot in the picture was the effort being made in many Protestant Episcopal churches to develop choirs, often including boys, that were dedicated to worship and not to self-glory. A leader in American church

## Lutkin

music, Peter C. Lutkin (1858-1931), was a product of an Episcopal choir school in Chicago. He served as a church organist at St. James when he was fourteen.

Lutkin was one of the many musicians and ministers who recognized the need for improvement and one of the few who did something about the situation. Among other contributions to church music, he established a department of church music in the Northwestern University School of Music shortly before the turn of the century. The department became a strong factor in the dissemination of a practical philosophy of church music. Lutkin taught, lectured, and wrote to promote his concepts of music and worship. He was himself an excellent church musician and a good composer. While not a Methodist, he worked in the preparation of the *Methodist Hymnal* of 1905 and served Methodist churches in numerous other capacities. He was also on the Protestant Episcopal Hymnal Commission. The choral program at Northwestern University gave careful attention to the needs of the church; Lutkin's famous a cappella choir had an extensive repertoire of religious music.

## Pratt

Waldo Seldon Pratt (1857-1939) spent most of his life as a lecturer at Hartford Theological Seminary. He attained fame as a musician and musicologist. He published a tiny book that had an effect upon church music far out of proportion to its size. *Musical Ministries in the Church* (New York: G. Schirmer, 1901) appeared in five editions, the last in 1923. Pratt discussed the weaknesses of Protestant church music and offered practical suggestions for eliminating them. A great deal of the progress made since 1901 has been, at least in part, based upon the concepts expressed in his book.

## Christiansen

F. Melius Christiansen (1871-1955) was appointed head of the music department at St. Olaf's College, Northfield, Minnesota, in 1903. His choir soon established a solid reputation for its interpretations of great liturgical music, much of it derived from Lutheran sources and arranged by Christiansen. Many church musicians studied at St. Olaf's or under Dr. Christiansen at one of the many institutes and workshops in which he participated.

## Parker

Horatio W. Parker (1863-1919) was a successful organist, director, editor, and teacher. While his compositions have lost much of their popularity they established new standards of quality upon which his successors might build. His oratorio *Hora Novissima* is occasionally performed today.

## Douglas

Winfred Douglas (1867-1944) did not permit poor health to keep him from living a full rich life. He did much to restore interest in liturgical music—for the congregation as well as for ministers and musicians. He was ordained a priest in the Protestant Episcopal Church and served in that capacity. Of all his numerous writings, *Church Music in History and Practice* (1937) is perhaps the most significant. (The book was republished in 1962 with an additional chapter written by Leonard Ellinwood.) His influence was greatly broadened because he gave freely of his time and talents to workshops and conferences. Several of his tunes and arrangements are in common use. "In dulci jubilo," with the words "Good Christian men, rejoice" is in most modern hymnals.

## Noble

T. Tertius Noble (1867-1953), like Horatio Parker, was a successful organist, director, editor, and teacher. His compositions attained great popularity, and a few are still sung occasionally. He served the Protestant Episcopal Church as a member of the Hymnal and Church Music Commission.

## doldrums and excitement

Church music between 1912 and 1925 was in the doldrums. The world was involved in fighting and recovering from a great war. No books of any particular value were published, except possibly *Music in the History of the Western Church* by Edward Dickinson in 1913 and *Worship and Music* by George Gardner in 1918. But the years since 1925 have been filled with exciting events, many of a strongly affirmative nature. These events become even more significant when interpreted in the light of changes in Protestant theology.

It should be emphasized that relatively little actual progress in church music was made between 1900 and 1925 despite the efforts of Pratt, Lutkin, Parker, and others, partially because the concepts they promoted and the philosophies they followed were designed for and applied to large congregations, particularly those of the more conservative denominations.

## small churches

Thousands and thousands of small congregations continued to wander along, using music—if at all—in a hit-or-miss fashion. The number of church members who benefited from an effective program of music was infinitesimally small.

People like to sing; people enjoy listening to music. The average congregation was not content, therefore, with nothing and proceeded to fill the void with songs and anthems that

## extremes

were often of doubtful value. The gap between the music of the Baptist, Christian, and Methodist churches of Podunk and that of St. James Episcopal Church of Metropolis was too great to be bridged without the efforts of many leaders over a period of many years.

### Methodist efforts

One of the first significant moves in this direction was made by a group of Methodist ministers and musicians in the early 1920's. A series of three conferences on church music was held in Rushville, Indiana, the first in 1921. A symposium consisting of lectures given at the conference was edited by John Mann Walker and published in 1923 by Abingdon Press.

### McCutchan and Thomas

Two of the lecturers, Robert G. McCutchan (1877-1958) and Edith Lovell Thomas (1878-), were to contribute greatly to the development of an effective church-music program during the succeeding three decades, McCutchan in the area of hymnody and Miss Thomas in music in Christian education. McCutchan was editor of *The Methodist Hymnal* (1935). His handbook (*Our Hymnody*) for the hymnal was published in 1937. He wrote numerous articles and books on his favorite subject, hymns and hymn tunes.

Miss Thomas was often almost alone in her efforts to promote sensible, lucid music for use in Christian education. Proof that she succeeded can be found in the improving quality of music heard today in most Protestant church schools. Her book, *Music in Christian Education* (Nashville: Abingdon Press, 1953) was the result of a lifetime of experience.

A veritable deluge of articles about church music and worship in general appeared in both religious and secular publications during the twenties. Of the few books published during the same period, *Church Music and Worship* (New York:

### Harper

The Abingdon Press, 1924) was the most influential. The author, Earl E. Harper (1895-), is an enthusiastic musician-turned-minister, who has actively promoted his suggestions for a practical, church-wide program of music for thirty years and is still going strong. Among other ideas, he advocated the development of children's and youth choirs wherever possible. Only a very few churches had such a program, despite its worth having been shown by Elizabeth Van Fleet Vosseller as early as 1900. She described her work in *The Use of a Children's Choir in the Church* (New York: H. W. Gray Company, 1907), a book that contains concepts still practical today.

Harper has served in many capacities—minister, teacher, administrator, lecturer, writer, and editor. He was active in the work of the commission that produced *The Methodist Hymnal* of 1935 and is now chairman of the Executive-Editorial Committee of the hymnal committee, which is presently revising the hymnal. He was primarily responsible for the organization in 1928 of an official commission to study music and worship in the church.

### other Methodist efforts

A number of other persons connected with The Methodist Church or with Methodist schools were involved in the developments of the twenties. Edward S. Ninde (1866-1935) added to knowledge and interest in hymns with his book *The Story of the American Hymn* (New York: The Abingdon Press, 1921). Carl F. Price (1881-1948) composed tunes and wrote, taught, and lectured about hymns and hymn tunes. Reginald McCall's (1878-1954) writings culminated in his book *Practical Church School Music* (New York: The Abingdon Press, 1932). Karl Pomeroy Harrington (1861-1953) served the church as a hymnologist and educator and wrote *Education in Church Music* (New York: The Century Company, 1931). Frank J. Metcalf (1865-1945), was interested primarily in hymn tunes, as is shown by his books, *American Writers and Compilers of Sacred Music* (New York: The Abingdon Press, 1925) and *Stories of Hymn Tunes* (New York: The Abingdon Press, 1928). H. Augustine Smith (1874-1954), teacher and author, wrote *Lyric Religion* (New York: The Century Company, 1931) and served as editor of *The New Church Hymnal*, published in 1937.

## Southern Baptist pioneering

The Southern Baptists were the first denomination to develop a planned, church-wide program of music. The excitement of the twenties resulted in the appointment in 1935 of a music editor for publications of the Sunday School Board. A study of church music needs and conditions was begun in 1937. As a result of this study statewide programs for improvement of church and Sunday-school music were started in 1939. In 1941 a church music department was created by the Sunday School Board. The goal of all this activity was a continuing program of education that would slowly but surely develop a more effective kind of music in worship and education. When the condition of music in the Southern Baptist Church in 1935 is compared with the situation today great improvement can easily be seen.

The Methodists and the Baptists were not alone in their efforts to bring life to church music. Other denominations showed their interest in various ways and with varying degrees of success. For example, the Presbyterian Church in the U. S. A. appointed a commission on music and worship in 1925 which has continued intermittently since that time. The Protestant Episcopal Church established a joint commission on church music in 1919.

## choir schools

Two nondenominational schools devoted to the training of church musicians were founded just two years apart. John F. Williamson (1887-) started the Westminster Choir College in 1926 while serving the Westminster Presbyterian Church, Dayton, Ohio. The college moved to Ithaca, New York, in 1929 and then to Princeton, New Jersey, in 1932. Clarence Dickinson (1873-) organized a school of sacred music at Union Theological Seminary, New York City, in 1928. Graduates of the two schools sometimes disagree, but they have accomplished a great deal in promoting a better kind of church music. Both Williamson and Dickinson have retired, the former in 1958 and the latter in 1945, but their great influence continues to be felt.

## Davison

Archibald T. Davison (1883-) resembles Waldo S. Pratt in that he has attained stature in several academic areas. His *Protestant Church Music in America* (New York: E. C. Schirmer Music Company, 1933) and *Church Music, Illusion and Reality* (Cambridge: Harvard University Press, 1952) are the products of a lifetime of lecturing and writing in an unceasing effort to promote his concepts of good church music. Davison, like the Englishman Robert Bridges, is uncompromising in his demand for purity and for the elimination from worship of anything sacrilegious or secular. His ideals are perhaps unattainable, but like Bridges, his courage and ability have enabled others to move more easily toward attainment of those ideals.

## Hymn Society

The Hymn Society of America has had much to do with the writing, editing, publishing, and use of hymns since its founding in 1923. The society's members represent all religious beliefs and many professions. The promotion of hymn festivals has proved to be one of its most effective devices for making America hymn conscious. The society publishes a monthly bulletin, *The Hymn*, and valuable *Papers* from time to time.

## A. G. O.

The American Guild of Organists was founded in 1896 and has increasingly affected the music of all Christendom until today it is a powerful factor in church life. Most of the men and women who have been influential in church music since 1925 have been members of A. G. O.

### organists and the church

Organists and their music have generally been an asset to the church. On occasions their concert ambitions have been known to interfere with worship. Just as quartets and choirs of the period from 1880 to 1920 were interested in performance rather than worship, so were some of the organists of that period inclined to play for the glory of themselves and their listeners rather than for the glory of God. The attitudes expressed by Pratt, Lutkin, and a few others eventually made an impression upon organists—but only after A. G. O. became an effective organization. Personal jealousies were a factor in delaying the guild's attainment of goals outlined in the "Declaration of the Religious Principle of the American Guild of Organists," which states emphatically that the organist and everyone and everything related to the music of the church must serve "For the greater glory of God . . . ." Sincere Guild members now look with real concern upon organists who do not follow this precept.

### The Diapason

Closely associated with the guild and constantly striving for the same ends is the organists' periodical *The Diapason*.

Its files reveal the missionary efforts of dedicated church musicians to bring about a proper union of music and worship.

The guild and *The Diapason* have always been interested in developing better organs as well as better music and better

*insanity*

musicians. Mechanical improvements of the late nineteenth and early twentieth centuries proved, however, to be a mixed blessing because they made possible the "orchestral" organ which became a monstrous parody upon its ancestors. It is fortunate that a few builders and organists retained their sanity; it was their courage and strength that finally brought an abrupt shift toward the tonal and musical concepts of the eighteenth century. Organs and organ music had degenerated to a dangerously low point in the early part of the

*theater organs*

century. The theater organ of the twenties was a fearful and wonderful creation; it threatened for a time to become the arbiter of standards in building and performance. It may well be that the advent of sound film and the resultant death of the theater organ was a basic factor in the return of sanity.

*return to sanity*

Since 1950 builders and organists have combined forces to design instruments that use the best from all centuries. Composers too are developing a composite style based upon both polyphonic and harmonic devices but using twentieth-century concepts of tonality and technique. The brave musicians who first ventured into this new area of composition were rather ignored until the recent revolution in organ construction. There are those who believe that Albert Schweitzer's efforts to focus attention upon Bach's music played as Bach played it may have had much to do with current trends.

*small pipe organs*

One of the most significant developments in modern organ building is the perfecting of small—three to seven ranks—pipe organs which have excellent tone and which serve the small church well. Organists delight in playing a fine instrument of seventy-five or more ranks, but they are not at all reluctant to explore the beauties of less expensive pipe organs.

Two instruments other than the pipe organ deserve atten-

*reed organ*

tion. The first, the reed organ, appeared in Europe about 1800; American manufacture started about 1820. The Mason and Hamlin became America's most popular parlor and small church instrument between 1855 and 1900 and retained its place in the church until the 1940's. Very few are in use today.

*electronic organ*

The second instrument, the so-called electronic organ, first appeared just prior to World War II. Because of its portability, and for other nonmusical reasons, the electronic instrument was placed in American Armed Forces chapels and thereby received a great amount of publicity. Numerous similar instruments have been introduced by other companies since the war.

In the hands of a competent organist certain "concert" model electronic instruments can be made to serve quite effectively, provided their assets are emphasized and their liabilities ignored. There is considerable feeling among church musicians that the best tone the instrument can produce does not compare favorably with that of the pipe organ. Small-sized electronic instruments, including spinets, are too limited in tonal variety and overall effectiveness to serve the church well. A modern three or four rank pipe organ costs about the same as the better electronic instruments and is considered by many to be a much better church instrument. The place of the electronic organ will not be determined for some time.

Between 1936 and 1950 relatively little of real significance was actually accomplished in church music. Wars and rumors *consolidation* of wars held the world's attention. About all that could be done was to consolidate the gains of the twenties. Several new "official" hymnals were published. Most reflected in some degree the attitudes toward music and worship that Pratt first enunciated in 1901 and that were elaborated upon by Lutkin, Harper, and others. The only startling event was the invention and popularization of the previously mentioned electronic organ.

A few books of real significance were published between 1929 and 1949. As is often the case, their effect was delayed. *Music and Worship* (Bryn Mawr, Pa.: The Oliver Ditson Company, 1929), written by W. S. Swisher, is a very small, extremely caustic book that seems to strive for the ideals Davison expressed so well a few years later.

Winfred Douglas' *Church Music in History and Practice* should be mentioned again. Its influence during this time of *Benson* growth was considerable. Louis F. Benson (1855-1930) is thought by many to have been America's greatest hymnologist. *The Hymnody of the Christian Church* (1927; reprinted, Richmond, Va.: John Knox Press, 1956) is one of the most valuable books of his and later generations. He edited hymnals, wrote and translated hymns, lectured, and otherwise worked unceasingly to spread his own great enthusiasm far and wide. His *The English Hymn* (1915; reprinted, John Knox Press, 1962) is a definitive and scholarly work.

104

### other authors

W. J. Finn (1881-1961) attained considerable stature as director of the Paulist Choristers, a choir of men and boys that sang for Old St. Mary's Catholic Church in Chicago. *The Art of the Choral Conductor* (Boston: C. C. Birchard and Company, 1939) is still a standard text. He wrote four other books on singing, church music, and conducting. His first book, a *Manual of Church Music*, was published in 1905 and the last, *The Conductor Raises His Baton*, in 1944.

### Ninde and Foote

Two books about hymns appeared about the same time: E. S. Ninde's *Nineteen Centuries of Christian Song* (Westwood, N. J.: Fleming H. Revell Company, 1938), and *Three Centuries of American Hymnody* (1940; reprinted: Hamden, Conn.: The Shoe String Press, 1961), which was the culminating work of Henry Wilder Foote (1875- ).

### Hjortsvang

A valuable, down to earth book, *The Amateur Choir Director*, by Carl Hjortsvang (1905- ), (Nashville: Abingdon Press, 1941) was an early attempt to give aid to untrained musicians who wished to serve their church. The book still serves effectively.

### the Dickinsons

Helen (1875-1957) and Clarence Dickinson collaborated with P. A. Wolfe to compile a series of worship services in which all materials used are related. The result is an inexpensive book full of workable ideas. The title is indicative of its contents: *The Choir Loft and the Pulpit* (New York: H. W. Gray Company, 1943).

### Shields

The concern felt by educators for proper use of music was expressed in the title of a successful book written by Elizabeth

Shields: *Music in the Religious Growth of Children* (Nashville: Abingdon Press, 1943).

Three effective and very different books appeared in 1948.

### Jacobs

Ruth Krehbiel Jacobs (1897-1960), founder of *The Choristers Guild*, published the first of her two books dealing with the practical aspects of church music for children, *The Successful Children's Choir*, in 1948 (Chicago: H. T. FitzSimons). The monthly *Choristers Guild Letter* sent to guild members since 1949 contains much valuable information about methods and materials for use in the religious training of children. Mrs. Jacobs died suddenly while conducting a children's choir festival in Oklahoma City, Oklahoma. Since her death her husband, Arthur Leslie Jacobs, continued as editor of the *Letter* until 1963, when poor health forced him to resign. Federal Lee Whittlesey replaced him as editor. Mrs. Jacobs' second book, *The Children's Choir* (Rock Island, Ill.: Augustana Book Concern, 1948), was based upon materials found in the *Letter*.

### Kettring

Donald D. Kettring's (1907-) *Steps Toward a Singing Church* (Philadelphia: The Westminster Press, 1948) is a detailed study of the promotion, organization, and maintenance of a complete music program in a large church. The ideas presented are not theories; he wrote from his and others' experiences.

### Clokey

Joseph W. Clokey (1890-1960) was well known for his teaching and composing. His very small book, *In Every Corner Sing* (New York: Morehouse-Barlow Company, 1945), reflects a lifetime of work as an organist-director in small churches. The booklet should be read by every minister, church musician, and music committeeman.

Clokey is one of several Americans who have composed much excellent organ music in recent years. Among this group are Seth Bingham (1882-); Garth Edmundson (1895-); David McK. Williams (1887-); Everett Titcomb (1884-); Healey Willan (1880-), an English-born Canadian; and Leo Sowerby (1895-).

## the fuming fifties

The years since 1950 have been rich, indeed. Only time will determine how much of what is happening is fundamental and how much is superficial. In some respects the fifties seem to have been a time of re-evaluation of standards, purposes, philosophies and attitudes. For example, the multiple choir program advocated so strongly in the twenties and thirties had gotten a bit out of hand. The goal seemed to be to have as many show-piece choirs as possible, without regard for the need, and often in violation of the basic purposes of a choir. During the last several years a much better perspective has been attained as a result of efforts by church musicians and Christian educators to learn more about one another and to develop a comprehensive program of music in worship and Christian nurture.

Many factors have contributed to the developments since

## workshops

1950. Perhaps the most significant single item has been the prairie-fire growth of workshops, conferences, and schools for in-service training of musicians, ministers, and educators. Since 1955 the number of such ventures has increased from a dozen or so to many dozens—perhaps even hundreds. Two major denominations, the Southern Baptists and the Methodists, maintain central offices for the promotion of church-wide

## NaFOMM

music programs. The National Fellowship of Methodist Musicians, which started in 1956 with one hundred members, now numbers almost two thousand churchmen whose only concern is the development of an effective program that will serve the entire church. Other denominations are considering the organization of similar groups.

◄ The need for a better understanding by ministers of the use of music in worship has long been recognized. Since 1925 seminaries have gradually introduced courses in church music and hymnology, but not until the fifties were they able to require these courses for graduation. If present trends continue all seminaries will soon enforce such a requirement. Many excellent books on worship which are now available can be used to supplement college training.

Denomination-owned publishing houses have made valuable contributions to church music during recent years. The appointment of music editors and the establishment of effective departments of music have enabled the houses to publish and promote good music and music books among their own members. Music Ministry, published by the Graded Press, Nashville (Methodist); The Church Musician, published by the Sunday School Board of the Southern Baptist Convention, Nashville; and The Journal of Church Music (Philadelphia: Journal of Church Music, Muhlenberg Press) are periodicals designed to serve those involved in the music of the church.

A large number of books on church music have been published since 1950. Time alone will determine their lasting effect.

## music and worship

The new—yet very old—concept that music should be an integral part of worship has had a pronounced effect upon hymns, hymnals, and congregational singing. The schism between advocates of "high-church" and "low-church" hymnody threatened for a time to become so wide that it could not be bridged. Differences within denominations became greater than differences between denominations. It is fortunate that the trend seems to be reversed and moving toward recognition of the needs of all people.

## congregational music

The most useful device for broadening the standards of congregational music has been twofold. First, many fine "official" church hymnals which include a wide range of materials have been compiled, and second, many groups are using hymn services, congregational rehearsals, hymn festivals, study courses, hymn-of-the-month plans, hymn sermons, and other devices to bring the people to a higher level of understanding and appreciation of effective congregational music.

## commercial influence

The problems of congregational music have recently been complicated by the addition of a factor not present in past years. Radio, phonographs, and television provide the purveyors of commercialized "religious" music a direct line into the lives of millions of people. Songs of a pseudo-sacred type are heard with embarrassing frequency on programs devoted to currently popular music. There is a great need to combat the influence of low-calibre, sometimes sacrilegious music by offering the people something that is not only better but actually more attractive. The dross in church music cannot be removed by issuing decrees. The answer lies in a continuous program of education and salesmanship.

Hymnals published since 1930 contain many hymns and tunes of twentieth century writers. Again time will determine

## hymn writers

which ones will last. A few writers have already proved themselves in terms of quality. Henry van Dyke (1852-1933), preacher, teacher, foreign minister, and scholar is firmly established by his "Joyful, joyful, we adore Thee," which he wrote for the principal theme in the last movement of Beethoven's *Ninth Symphony.*

Katharine Lee Bates (1859-1929) wrote her most famous hymn, "O beautiful for spacious skies," in 1893. It may well be considered a twentieth-century hymn in spirit and mood, however.

Frank Mason North (1850-1935) wrote one of the few hymns concerned with problems of urban life, "Where cross the crowded ways of life." His other hymns, although less well known, reflect his great concern for people.

Jay T. Stocking (1870-1936) may well be remembered for the one hymn he wrote, "O Master Workman of the race." William Pierson Merrill (1867-1954, "Rise up, O men of God") and Henry Hallam Tweedy (1868-1953, "Eternal God, whose power upholds") contributed several fine hymns that may be long-lived.

## Tillett

Wilbur F. Tillett (1854-1936) was one of America's great hymnologists. He served on three Methodist hymnal commissions and was chairman of the tune committee for the 1935 *Methodist Hymnal.* He wrote *Our Hymns and Their Authors* (Nashville: Publishing House of the Methodist Episcopal Church, South, 1889), an authoritative work. His "O Son of God incarnate" is a popular hymn of considerable value.

Others who should be mentioned are: Earl Marlatt (1892-,

"Spirit of Life, in this new dawn") and Harry Emerson Fosdick (1878-, "God of grace and God of glory").

A few twentieth-century hymn tunes may stand the test of time, many others may not. Some recent hymnals contain almost no new tunes; others contain several, but only a small handful of new tunes have attained more than local acceptance. It is interesting and perhaps significant that early nineteenth-century American folk music is gradually finding a place in "official" hymnals.

## music for choirs

One of the most encouraging indications of resurgent American church music is the increase in quantity as well as quality of usable sacred choral compositions. Leading composers are giving considerable attention to this long-neglected area. While the permanent value of religious music composed during the last two decades cannot be determined, at least some of it is of excellent quality and in good taste. The percentage of good music is increasing, but it is still embarrassingly small. Only as congregations, ministers, choirs, and directors become more demanding of composers and publishers will the percentage continue to increase.

A list of contemporary American composers who have written sacred choral music would be quite long and of no particular value. A few men, however, have become established so firmly that they should at least be mentioned.

| | |
|---|---|
| Healey Willan | Virgil Thomson |
| Leo Sowerby | Richard Purvis |
| Samuel Barber | H. Everett Titcomb |
| Alan Hovhaness | Joseph Clokey |
| Randall Thompson | Lloyd Pfautsch |
| William Schuman | Austin C. Lovelace |

111

# Now and Then

Three groups of people have always been concerned with and affected by church music—the clergy, the musicians, and the congregation. The use of music in worship and Christian nurture has been determined by the attitudes, knowledge, and ability of all three. Usually the clergy has been dominant, occasionally the congregation, and rarely the musicians. Because each has a viewpoint radically different from the other two, lines of communication have been flimsy and co-operation weak.

Recently a fourth group appeared—those concerned primarily with Christian education—and the picture has become even more complicated as the minister, the musician, and the educator find themselves inadvertently or intentionally competing for the time and attention of the congregation.

Problems of church music have been made increasingly obvious by the continuing reluctance of many well-trained musicians to have anything to do with the composing or performing of sacred music. There are more symphony orchestras and community instrumental and choral groups today than at any time in past years. Their concern is primarily secular, however, even when they perform great sacred masterpieces.

The situation has been further confounded by the enormous strides school music has taken since 1925. Almost every American public and parochial school has an effective instrumental and choral program.

Mention sacred music to an average group of American youth. Some will respond with blank stares. Some will mention "He," "The Man Upstairs," or other examples of commercialized "religious" music. Some will break into "Gimme that old-time religion." A few will think of "The church's one foundation" or "O Master Workman of the race."

The times are not without hope, however. There are many signs of a revitalized, resurgent kind of church music that will eventually regain its dominant place in American and European culture.

1. Several Protestant denominations are in the process of developing music programs that will serve the needs of all their people. Emphasis is being placed upon the use of music in Christian nurture as well as in worship.

2. Composers are giving attention to the need of churches and church schools for much good, easy music.

3. Church-related schools and theological seminaries are encouraging ministers, musicians, and educators to study hymnology, music in worship, and music in Christian nurture.

4. Some state-supported colleges and universities are improving their offerings in church music.

5. A whole new generation of composers who are strongly interested in church music is coming to the fore. Some will say that the genius of Leo Sowerby has been a prime factor in this development.

6. Literally hundreds of in-service church music schools and workshops are held every year for all who are concerned in any way with music in worship and Christian nurture.

7. Organizations not primarily concerned with church music, such as the Music Teachers National Association, the

Music Educators National Conference, and the National Association of Teachers of Singing are giving considerable attention to church music. MTNA has a permanent and active church-music committee. NATS has sponsored studies related to sacred solo literature.

8. Recent hymnal revisions have, on the whole, produced better hymnals. One of the most significant is the Lutheran *Service Book and Hymnal* (1958). It is truly an American hymnal, containing the offerings of composers and authors of all denominations and races and from all generations.

9. The emergence of the career church musician, with training in church polity, theology, and church administration, has done much to break down the barriers between musician and minister. Many such musicians have seen the need for leadership and have given generously of themselves in an effort to serve the whole church. The Pratts, Lutkins, and Harpers of the early 1900's have been multiplied many times over.

10. Demands for guidance have resulted in the publication since 1950 of more books and articles about church music than were published in the preceding fifty years. In addition to new books, several fine books have been re-published.

11. The growth between 1925 and 1950 of an effective school music program literally forced the church to re-evaluate its music. Children, youth, and adults could not be expected to participate wholeheartedly in a church music program whose shortcomings had become increasingly obvious.

12. Training given in recent years in cultural studies—especially the fine arts—by public institutions of learning seems to have declined in quality. The situation is right for the church to regain its old position as the cultural leader of the world.

13. The National Council of Churches of Christ has given

impetus to the study of music and worship by means of its effective Department of Worship and the Arts.

14. Last, but far from least, individual congregations, groups of churches within specific geographical areas and entire denominations are increasingly aware of the need to provide financial support for the music program. One fact alone can justify the foregoing statement: Every important pipe organ company is twelve to thirty months behind in completing contracted installations.

The present is exciting, and the future is bright. The day should soon come when sacred music will again be at least equal to secular music in quality and quantity. Beauty and holiness will exist in proper perspective and the holiness of beauty will be a reality instead of a dream oftentimes tinged with nightmare horrors.

# Additional Readings

More detailed information may be found in the following books. Repeated titles are abbreviated.

## A. SPECIFIC

### Chapter I

Gradenwitz, Peter. *The Music of Israel*. New York: W. W. Norton & Company, 1949.

Idelsohn, Abraham. *Jewish Music*. New York: Tudor Publishing Company, 1946.

*New Oxford History of Music, The*. Vol. I, *Ancient and Oriental Music*. Edited by Egdon Willez. London: Oxford University Press, 1957.

Sachs, Curt. *The Rise of Music in the Ancient World*. New York: W. W. Norton & Company, 1943.

### Chapter II

Grout, Donald J. *A History of Western Music*. New York: W. W. Norton & Company, 1960.

Harman, Alec. *Mediaeval and Early Renaissance Music*. New York: Oxford University Press, 1958.

McKinney, Howard D., and Anderson, William R. *Music in History*. New York: American Book Company, 1940.

*New Oxford History of Music, The*. Vol. II, *Early Medieval Music—Up to 1300*. Edited by Dom Anselm Hughes. London: Oxford University Press, 1954.

Reese, Gustave. *Music in the Middle Ages*. New York: W. W. Norton & Company, 1940.

## Chapter III

Grout. *A History of Western Music.*

Harman, Alec and Milner, Anthony. *Late Renaissance and Baroque Music.* New York: Oxford University Press, 1959.

Harman. *Mediaeval and Early Renaissance Music.*

McKinney and Anderson. *Music in History.*

*New Oxford History of Music, The.* Vol. III, *Ars Nova and the Renaissance—1300-1540.* Edited by Dom Anselm Hughes and Gerald Abraham. London: Oxford University Press, 1960.

Reese, Gustave. *Music in the Renaissance.* New York: W. W. Norton & Company, 1954.

## Chapter IV

Bukofzer, Manfred F. *Music in the Baroque Era.* New York: W. W. Norton & Company, 1947.

Grout. *A History of Western Music.*

Harmon and Milner. *Late Renaissance and Baroque Music.*

Lang, Paul H. *Music in Western Civilization.* New York: W. W. Norton & Company, 1941.

## Chapter V

Grout. *A History of Western Music.*

Lang. *Music in Western Civilization.*

McKinney and Anderson. *Music in History.*

## Chapter VI

Chase, Gilbert. *America's Music.* New York: McGraw-Hill Book Company, 1955.

Ellinwood, Leonard. *The History of American Church Music.* New York: Morehouse-Gorham Company, 1953.

Foote, Henry W. *Three Centuries of American Hymnody.* Hamden, Conn.: The Shoe String Press, 1961. First edition, Harvard University Press, 1940.

Howard, John T. *Our American Music.* 3rd edition. New York:

The Thomas Y. Crowell Company, 1946. First ed. 1929. Revised edition, 1955.

**Chapter VII**

Grout. *A History of Western Music.*

Lang. *Music in Western Civilization.*

McKinney and Anderson. *Music in History.*

**Chapter VIII**

Chase. *America's Music.*

Ellinwood. *The History of American Church Music.*

Foote. *Three Centuries of American Hymnody.*

Howard. *Our American Music.*

**Chapter IX**

Grout. *A History of Western Music.*

Hanson, Peter S., editor. *An Introduction to Twentieth Century Music.* Rockleigh, N. J.: Allyn and Bacon, Inc., 1961.

Lang. *Music in Western Civilization.*

Mellers, Wilfred H. *Romanticism and the 20th Century.* New York: Oxford University Press, 1957.

**Chapter X**

Chase. *America's Music.*

Cox, Norman W. *Encyclopedia of Southern Baptists.* 2 vols. Nashville: Broadman Press, 1958.

Ellinwood. *The History of American Church Music.*

Foote. *Three Centuries of American Hymnody.*

Hanson. *An Introduction to Twentieth Century Music.*

Howard. *Our American Music.*

**Chapter XI**

Bukofzer. *Music in the Baroque Era.*

Etherington, C. L. *Protestant Worship Music.* New York: Holt, Rinehart & Winston, Inc., 1962.

Grout. *A History of Western Music*.

Reese. *Music in the Renaissance*.

## B. GENERAL

Bailey, Albert E. *The Gospel in Hymns*. New York: Charles Scribner's Sons, 1944.

Benson, Louis F. *The English Hymn*. Richmond, Va.: John Knox Press, 1960.

_____. *The Hymnody of the Christian Church*. Richmond, Va.: John Knox Press, 1956. Reprinted 1962. First edition, George H. Doran Company, 1927.

Douglas, Winfred. *Church Music in History and Practice*. New York: Charles Scribner's Sons, 1940. Revised edition, 1962.

Haeussler, Armin. *The Story of Our Hymns*. St. Louis: Eden Publishing House, 1952.

*Hymns Ancient and Modern, Historical Edition*. London: William Clowes and Sons, Ltd., 1909.

Lightwood, J. T. *The Music of the Methodist Hymn Book*. London: The Epworth Press, 1935. Revised edition, 1955.

McCutchan, Robert G. *Our Hymnody*. Nashville: Abingdon Press, 1937.

*Papers of the Hymn Society of America*, 475 Riverside Drive, New York 27, N. Y.

Patrick, M. *Four Centuries of Scottish Psalmody*. London: Oxford University Press, 1949.

Phillips, C. Henry. *The Singing Church*. London: Faber & Faber Ltd., 1945.

Routley, Eric. *The Church and Music*. London: Gerald Duckworth and Company, Ltd., 1950.

_____. *The Music of Christian Hymnody*. London: Independent Press, Ltd., 1957.

Ryden, Ernest E. *The Story of Christian Hymnody*. Rock Island, Ill.: Augustana Book Concern, 1959.

Sachs, Curt. *Our Musical Heritage*. Englewood Cliffs, N. J.: Prentice-Hall, Inc., 1955. First edition, 1948.

Stevenson, R. *Music Before the Classic Era*. London: Macmillan and Company, Ltd., 1958. First edition, 1955.

Squire, Russel N. *Church Music*. St. Louis: The Bethany Press, 1962.

# Index

127